LIFE IN THE UK TEST

ALL IN ONE

STUDY GUIDE WITH FULL HANDBOOK

AND PRACTICE QUESTIONS

2023 Edition

CITIZENSHIP EDUCATION

ISBN: 9798373535069

Introduction to the 2023 Edition   10

The 2023 Test   11

Chapter 1 - The Values and Principles of the UK   15
   Becoming a permanent resident   16

Chapter 2 - What is the UK?   18

Chapter 3 - A Long and Illustrious History   20
   Early Britain   20
   The Romans   21
   The Anglo-Saxons   22
   The Vikings   23
   The Norman Conquest   24
   The Middle Ages   25
   War at home and abroad   25
   The Black Death   27
   Legal and Political Changes   28
   A Distinct Identity   29
   The Wars of The Roses   31
   The Tudors and Stuarts   32
   Queen Elizabeth I   34
   The Reformation in Scotland and Mary, Queen of Scots   35
   Exploration, Poetry and Drama 36
   James VI and I   37
   The King James Bible   37
   Ireland   37
   The Rise of Parliament   38
   The Beginning of the English Civil War   39
   Oliver Cromwell & The English Republic   40

The Restoration   41
Isaac Newton (1643-1727)   42
A Catholic King   43
The Glorious Revolution   44
Constitutional Monarchy – The Bill of Rights   45
A Growing Population   47
'The Act' or Treaty of Union in Scotland   47
The Prime Minister   48
The Rebellion of the Clans   48
Robert Burns (1759-96)   49
The Enlightenment   49
The Industrial Revolution   50
Richard Arkwright (1732-92)   52
Sake Dean Mahomet (1759-1851)   52
The Slave Trade   52
The American War of Independence   54
War with France   55
The Union Flag   55
The Victorian Age   56
Trade and Industry   57
Isambard Kingdom Brunel (1806-59)   58
The Crimean War   58
Florence Nightingale (1820-1910)   59
The Right to Vote   60
Emmeline Pankhurst (1858-1928)   61
The Future of the Empire   62
Rudyard Kipling (1865-1936)   63
The First World War   64
The Partition of Ireland   66
The Inter-War Period   67

The Second World War   68
Winston Churchill (1874-1965)   71
Alexander Fleming (1881-1955)   72
The Welfare State   72
Clement Attlee (1883-1967)   74
William Beveridge (1879-1963)   74
R A Butler (1902-82)   75
Dylan Thomas (1914-53)   75
Migration in Post-War Britain   76
Social change in the 1960s   76
Problem in the economy in the 1970s   80
Mary Peters (1939-)   81
Europe and the Common Market   81
Conservative government from 1979 to 1997   82
Margaret Thatcher (1925-2013)   82
Roald Dahl (1916-90)   83
Labour government from 1997 to 2010   83
Conflicts in Afghanistan and Iraq   84
Coalition government 2010 onwards   85

Chapter 4 - A Modern, Thriving Society   86
The UK Today   86
Languages and Dialects   87
Population   87
Ethnic Diversity   88
An Equal Society   88
Religion   89
Christian Churches   90
Patron Saints' Days   91
Customs and Traditions   92

Other Religious Festivals 93
Other Festivals and Traditions 94
Bank Holidays 96
Sport 97
Notable British Sportsmen and Women 98
Cricket 100
Football 101
Rugby 102
Horse Racing 102
Golf 102
Tennis 103
Water Sports 103
Motor Sports 104
Skiing 104
Arts and Culture 104
Theatre 108
Art 109
Notable British artists 110
Architecture 112
Fashion and Design 114
Literature 114
Notable Authors and Writers 115
British Poets 116
Leisure 118
Gardening 119
Shopping 119
Cooking and Food 120
Traditional Foods 120
British Film Industry 121
British Comedy 123

Television and Radio   124
Social Networking   126
Pubs and Night Clubs   126
Betting and Gambling   127
Pets   127
Places of Interest   127
UK Landmarks   128

Chapter 5 - The UK Government, the Law and Your
Role   131
The Development of British Democracy   131
The British Constitution   132
Constitutional Institutions   133
The Monarchy   133
The National Anthem   135
System of Government   136
The House of Commons   136
The House of Lords   137
Elections   138
The Prime Minister   139
The Cabinet   139
The Opposition   141
The Party System   141
The Civil Service   142
Local Government   143
Devolved Administrations   143
The Welsh Government   144
The Scottish Parliament   145
The Northern Ireland Assembly   145
The Media and Government   146

Who Can Vote? 147

The Electoral Register 148

Where to Vote 149

Standing for Office 150

The UK Parliament 150

The UK and International Institutions 151

The European Union 152

The Council of Europe 152

The United Nations 153

The North Atlantic Treaty Organization (NATO) 153

Respecting the Law 153

The Law in the UK 154

Terrorism and Extremism 158

The Judiciary 159

Criminal Courts 159

Magistrates' and Justice of the Peace Courts 160

Crown Courts and Sheriff Courts 160

Youth Courts 161

Civil Courts 161

The Small Claims Procedure 162

Legal Advice 163

Fundamental principles 164

Domestic violence 165

Female Genital Mutilation 166

Forced marriage 166

Income Tax 166

National Insurance 167

Getting a National Insurance Number 168

Driving 169

Your Role in the Community   170
Being a Good Neighbor   171
Getting Involved in Local Activities   172
Helping in Schools   172
School Governors and School Boards   173
Supporting Political Parties   174
Helping with Local Services   174
Blood and Organ Donation   175
Other Ways to Volunteer   175
Looking After the Environment   177

Practice Test 1   180

Practice Test 2   187

Practice Test 3   194

Practice Test 4   201

Practice Test 5   208

Practice Test 6   214

Practice Test 8   229

Practice Test 9   236

Practice Test 10   243

Answers to Practice Test 1   251

Answers to Practice Test 2   261

Answers to Practice Test 3   270

Answers to Practice Test 4   284

Answers to Practice Test 5   299

Answers to Practice Test 6   315

Answers to Practice Test 7   332

Answers to Practice Test 8   348

Answers to Practice Test 9   363

Answers to Practice Test 10   372

Introduction to the 2023 Edition

As the United Kingdom emerges from the Covid-19 pandemic, it is exciting to see a significant rise in the number of visitors to the country. The latest statistics show a staggering 95.5 million passenger arrivals into the UK, including returning UK residents. The UK government has also opened up the BN(O) immigration route, which received over 10,000 applications in the last year. It is clear that the UK remains a place where many thousands of people wish to visit, study, and reside.

Furthermore, the number of applications for British citizenship has also seen a significant increase in the year ending September 2022. With 183,414 applications, this is a 5% increase from 2019 prior to the pandemic. Non-EU nationals accounted for 136,736 of these applications, a 9% increase from 2019. Even more noteworthy is the increase in citizenship applications from EU nationals, accounting for 25% of all citizenship applications in the year ending September 2022, compared to 12% in 2016. This increase is likely a result of people seeking to confirm their status in the UK following the EU referendum and the UK's exit from the EU.

The UK government has also granted 185,857 grants of British citizenship in the year ending September 2022, a 17% increase from 2019 prior to the pandemic. This increase comes after a period of relative stability since 2014.

On a different note, the UK also mourned the loss

of Her Majesty the Queen last year, which means there will be a lot of changes. This includes the Life in the UK test questions, King Charles is now the UK's head of state, and the national anthem is now 'God Save The King.' There are also changes to the insignia seen on many everyday things, for instance, the Queen will be removed from the currency, stamps, and police emblems and replaced with the King's insignia.

Despite these changes, the system for being granted citizenship remains the same. Applicants must pass both the Life in the UK test as well as take an English test at least the 'B1' level. To assist with the preparation, there are plenty of resources available such as books packed with practice questions and answers that will help applicants understand the structure and content of the test. Overall, the UK continues to be an attractive destination for people from all over the world, and these recent statistics are a testament to that.

The 2023 Test

The questions are all multiple choice and come in a number of types. Some questions have 4 possible answers and you need to select one option A, B, C or D. For example:

Which date is boxing day?

A. 25th of December Each Year

B. 26th of December Each Year

C. 27th December Each Year

D. 29th December Each Year

Or you will be given a statement and asked whether it is is TRUE or False, for example:

Alfred Hitchcock was a famous film director?

Other questions will ask you to select two options: Which are the two houses of parliament?

A. The House of Lords

B. The House of Commons

C. The House of Windsor

D. The House of Representatives

The answers are towards the back of the book and include an explanation of the correct answer. You can use these to identify areas you need further study in. Where there is the option for two answers you must get both right in order to get the point for that question. Overall you must get at least 18 out of 24 questions correct in order to pass. That means there is a passing threshold of 75%.

You will have 45 minutes to answer all the questions. Remember this is a multiple choice test so if you are not sure at first simply move onto the next question and come back to it at the end.

Ensure you read the questions throughly and the you understand exactly what the question is asking.

The mock questions in this book prepare you for key aspects of British life, culture, and identity that may be covered in the official Life in the UK test. The handbook covers the following topics:

- The values and principles of the UK
- Democracy, including the political system and elections
- The rule of law, including civil, criminal, and public law
- Individual liberty and rights as a British citizen
- Tolerance of different faiths and beliefs in a multicultural society
- Participation in community life
- Understanding the geography and history of the UK, including the four countries that make it up and key historical events
- Life in the UK today, including customs, traditions, and popular culture
- The British constitution, government, and law, including rights and responsibilities as a citizen

You can book the Life in the UK test on the .gov website and there are test centers located throughout the UK. The course is £50 and evening and weekend slots are available. To prepare for the test, you can take free mock tests on liveintheuk.co.uk and take an online course that breaks down the handbook into bite-size lessons. The course is mobile-optimized and offers a learner dashboard to track progress and take online tests. We wish you the best of luck with the test and becoming a new British citizen! Welcome home!

Chapter 1 - The Values and Principles of the UK

All British citizens must respect the individual liberties, values and principles the UK was established upon. These values have evolved over 1000 years of British history, tradition and customs and are a fundamental part of what it means to be British.

The fundamental principles of British life include:

- Democracy
- The rule of law
- Individual liberty
- Tolerance of those with different faiths and beliefs
- Participation in community life

You will attend a citizenship ceremony where you will be granted citizenship by a local official, as a new citizen you will take a pledge to uphold the values above.

The official pledge is: 'I will give my loyalty to the United Kingdom and respect its rights and freedoms. I will uphold its democratic values. I will observe its laws faithfully and fulfil my duties and obligations as a British citizen.'

If you wish to be a permanent resident or citizen of the UK, you should:

• Obey the law and the spirit of the law
• Be respectful of the rights of other people, including their freedom of expression
• Look after and provide for you and your family
• Look after those in your community and the area you live in

As a British citizen you will have the RIGHT to:

• Freedom of belief and religion
• Freedom of speech
• Freedom from illegal discrimination
• A right to a fair trial
• A right to join in the elections

Becoming a permanent resident

To apply to become a permanent resident or citizen of the UK, you will need to:

• Speak and read English

· Have a good understanding of life in the UK.

There are currently two ways you can be tested on these requirements:

· Pass the Life in the UK test

AND

· Produce acceptable evidence of speaking and listening skills in English at B1 of the Common European Framework of Reference. This is equivalent to ESOL Entry Level 3. The requirements for citizenship applications may also change in the future.

Further details will be published on the UK Border Agency website and you should check the information on that website for current requirements before applying for settlement or citizenship.

Chapter 2 - What is the UK?

The UK is made up of England, Scotland, Wales and Northern Ireland. The rest of Ireland is an independent country. The official name of the country is the United Kingdom of Great Britain and Northern Ireland. 'Great Britain' refers only to England, Scotland and Wales, not to Northern Ireland. The words 'Britain', 'British Isles' or 'British', however, are used in this book to refer to everyone in the UK. There are also several islands which are closely linked with the UK but are not part of it: the Channel Islands and the Isle of Man.

These have their own governments and are called 'Crown dependencies'. There are also several British overseas territories in other parts of the world, such as St Helena and the Falkland Islands. They are also linked to the UK but are not part of it. The UK is governed by the parliament sitting in Westminster. Scotland, Wales and Northern Ireland also have parliaments or assemblies of their own, with devolved powers in defined areas.

Chapter 3 - A Long and Illustrious History

Early Britain

The first people to live in Britain were hunter-gatherers, in what we call the Stone Age. For much of the Stone Age, Britain was connected to the continent by a land bridge. People came and went, following the herds of deer and horses which they hunted. Britain only became permanently separated from the continent by the Channel about 10,000 years ago. The first farmers arrived in Britain 6,000 years ago. The ancestors of these first farmers probably came from south-east Europe. These people built houses, tombs and monuments on the land. One of these monuments, Stonehenge, still stands in what is now the English county of Wiltshire. Stonehenge was probably a special gathering place for seasonal ceremonies. Other Stone Age sites have also survived. Skara Brae on Orkney, off the north coast of Scotland, is the best preserved prehistoric village in northern Europe, and has helped archaeologists to understand more about how people lived near the end of the Stone Age.

Around 4,000 years ago, people learned to make bronze. We call this period the Bronze Age. People lived in roundhouses and buried their dead in tombs called round barrows. The people of the Bronze Age were accomplished metalworkers who made many beautiful objects in bronze and gold, including tools, ornaments and weapons. The Bronze Age was followed by the Iron Age, when people learned how to make weapons and tools out of iron. People still lived in roundhouses grouped together into larger settlements, and sometimes defended sites called hill forts. A very impressive hill fort can still be seen today at Maiden Castle, in the English county of Dorset. Most people were farmers, craft workers or warriors. The language they spoke was part of the Celtic language family. Similar languages were spoken across Europe in the Iron Age and related languages are still spoken today in some parts of Wales, Scotland and Ireland. The people of the Iron Age had a sophisticated culture and economy. They made the first coins to be minted in Britain, some inscribed with the names of Iron Age kings. This marks the beginnings of British history.

The Romans

Julius Caesar led a Roman invasion of Britain in 55 BC. This was unsuccessful and for nearly 100 years Britain remained separate from the Roman Empire. In AD 43 the Emperor Claudius led the Roman army in a new invasion. This time, there was resistance from some of the British tribes but the Romans were successful in occupying almost all of Britain. One of the tribal leaders who fought against the Romans was Boudicca, the queen of the Iceni in what is now eastern England. She is still remembered today and there is a statue of her on Westminster Bridge in London, near the Houses of Parliament. Areas of what is now Scotland were never conquered by the Romans, and the Emperor Hadrien built a wall in the north of England to keep out the Picts (ancestors of the Scottish people). Included in the wall were a number of forts. Parts of Hadrien's Wall, including the forts of Housesteads and Vindolanda, can still be seen. It is a popular area for walkers and is a UNESCO (United Nations Educational Scientific and Cultural Organization) World Heritage Site. The Romans remained in Britain for 400 years. They built roads and public buildings, created a structure of law, and introduced new plants and animals. It was during the 3rd and 4th centuries AD that the first Christian communities began to appear in Britain.

The Anglo-Saxons

The Roman army left Britain in AD 410 to defend other parts of the Roman Empire and never returned. Britain was again invaded by tribes from northern Europe: the Jutes, the Angles and the Saxons. The languages they spoke are the basis of modern-day English. Battles were fought against these invaders but, by about AD 600, Anglo-Saxon kingdoms were established in Britain. These kingdoms were mainly in what is now England. The burial place of one of the kings was at Sutton Hoo in modern Suffolk. This king was buried with treasure and armour, all placed in a ship which was then covered by a mound of earth. Parts of the west of Britain, including much of what is now Wales, and Scotland, remained free of Anglo-Saxon rule. The Anglo-Saxons were not Christians when they first came to Britain but, during this period, missionaries came to Britain to preach about Christianity. Missionaries from Ireland spread the religion in the north. The most famous of these were St Patrick, who would become the patron saint of Ireland, and St Columba, who founded a monastery on the island of Iona, off the coast of what is now Scotland. St Augustine led missionaries from Rome, who spread Christianity in the south. St Augustine became the first Archbishop of Canterbury.

The Vikings

The Vikings came from Denmark and Norway. They first visited Britain in AD 789 to raid coastal towns and take away goods and slaves. Then, they began to stay and form their own communities in the east of England and Scotland. The Anglo-Saxon kingdoms in England united under King Alfred the Great, who defeated the Vikings. Many of the Viking invaders stayed in Britain – especially in the east and north of England in an area known as the

Danelaw (many place names there, such as Grimsby and Scunthorpe come from the Viking languages). The Viking settlers mixed with local communities and some converted to Christianity. Anglo-Saxon kings continued to rule what is now England, except for a short period when there were Danish kings. The first of these was Cnut, also named Canute. In the north, the threat of attack by Vikings had encouraged the people to unite under one king, Kenneth MacAlpin. The term Scotland began to be used to describe that country.

The Norman Conquest

In 1066, an invasion led by William, the Duke of Normandy (in what is now northern France), defeated Harold, the Saxon king of England, at the Battle of Hastings. Harold was killed in the battle. William became king of England and is known as William the Conqueror. The battle is commemorated in a great piece of embroidery, known as the Bayeux tapestry, which can still be seen in France today.

The Norman Conquest was the last successful foreign invasion of England and led to many changes in government and social structures in England. Norman French, the language of the new ruling class influenced the development of the English language as we know it today. Initially the Normans also conquered Wales, but the Welsh gradually won territory back. The Scots and the

Normans fought on the border between England and Scotland; the Normans took over some land on the border but did not invade Scotland. William sent people all over England to draw up lists of all the towns and villages. The people who lived there, who owned the land and what animals they owned were also listed. This was called the Domesday Book. It still exists today and gives a picture of society in England just after the Norman Conquest.

Check that you understand

· The history of the UK before the Romans
· The impact of the Romans on British society
· The different groups that invaded after the Romans
· The importance of the Norman invasion in 1066

The Middle Ages

War at home and abroad

The period after the Norman Conquest up until about 1485 is called the Middle Ages (or the medieval period). It was a time of almost constant war. The English kings fought with the Welsh, Scottish and Irish noblemen for control of their lands. In Wales, the English were able to establish their rule. In 1284 King Edward I of England introduced the Statute of Rhuddlan, which annexed Wales to the Crown of England. Huge castles, including Conwy and Caenarvon, were built to maintain this power. By the middle of the 15th century the last Welsh rebellions had been defeated. English laws and the English language were introduced. In Scotland, the English kings were less successful. In 1314 the Scottish, led by Robert the Bruce, defeated the English at the Battle of Bannockburn, and Scotland remained unconquered by the English.

At the beginning of the Middle Ages, Ireland was an independent country. The English first went to Ireland as troops to help the Irish king and remained to build their own settlements. By 1200, the English ruled an area of Ireland known as the Pale, around Dublin. Some of the important lords in other parts of Ireland accepted the authority of the English king. During the Middle Ages, the English kings also fought a number of wars abroad. Many knights took part in the Crusades, in which European Christians fought for control of the Holy Land. English kings also fought a long war with France, called the Hundred Years War (even though it actually lasted 116 years). One of the most famous battles of the Hundred Years War was the Battle of Agincourt in 1415, where King Henry V's vastly outnumbered English army defeated the French. The English left France in the 1450s.

The Black Death

The Normans used a system of land ownership known as feudalism. The king gave land to his lords in return for help in war. Landowners had to send certain numbers of men to serve in the army. Some peasants had their own land but most were serfs. They had a small area of their lord's land where they could grow food. In return, they had to work for their lord and could not move away. The same system developed in southern Scotland. In the north of Scotland and Ireland, land was owned by members of the 'clans' (prominent families). In 1348, a disease, probably a form of plague, came to Britain. This was known as the Black Death. One third of the population of England died and a similar proportion in Scotland and Wales. This was one of the worst disasters ever to strike Britain. Following the Black Death, the smaller population meant there was less need to grow cereal crops. There were labour shortages and peasants began to demand higher wages. New social classes appeared, including owners of large areas of land (later called the gentry), and people left the countryside to live in the towns. In the towns, growing wealth led to the development of a strong middle class. In Ireland, the Black Death killed many in the Pale and, for a time, the area controlled by the English became smaller.

Legal and Political Changes

In the Middle Ages, Parliament began to develop into the institution it is today. Its origins can be traced to the king's council of advisers, which included important noblemen and the leaders of the Church. There were few formal limits to the king's power until 1215. In that year, King John was forced by his noblemen to agree to a number of demands. The result was a charter of rights called the Magna Carta (which means the Great Charter). The Magna Carta established the idea that even the king was subject to the law. It protected the rights of the nobility and restricted the king's power to collect taxes or to make and change laws. In future, the king would need to involve his noblemen in decisions. In England, parliaments were called for the king to consult his nobles, particularly when the king needed to raise money. The numbers attending Parliament increased and two separate parts, known as Houses were established. This nobility, great landowners and bishops sat in the House of Lords. Knights, who were usually smaller landowners, and wealthy people from towns and cities were elected to sit in the House of Commons. Only a small part of the population was able to join in electing the members of the Commons. A similar Parliament developed in Scotland. It had three Houses, called Estates: the lords, the commons and the clergy. This was also a time of development in the legal system. The principle that judges are independent of the government began to be established. In England, judges developed 'common law' by a process of precedence (that is, following previous decisions) and tradition. In Scotland, the legal system developed slightly differently and laws were 'codified' (that is, written down).

A Distinct Identity

The Middle Ages saw the development of a national culture and identity. After the Norman Conquest, the king and his noblemen had spoken Norman French and the peasants had continued to speak Anglo-Saxon. Gradually these two languages combined to become one English language. Some words in modern English – for example, 'park' and 'beauty' – are based on Norman French words. Other – for example, 'apple', 'cow' and 'summer' – are based on Anglo-Saxon words. In modern English there are often two words with very similar meanings, one from French and one from AngloSaxon. 'Demand' (French) and 'ask' (Anglo-Saxon) are examples. By 1400, in England, official documents were being written in English, and English had become the preferred language of the royal court and Parliament. In the years leading up to 1400, Geoffrey Chaucer wrote a series of poems in English about a group of people going to Canterbury on a pilgrimage. The people decided to tell each other stories on the journey, and the poems describe the travellers and some of the stories they told. This collection of poems is called The Canterbury Tales. It was one of the first books to be printed by William Caxton, the first person in England to print books using a printing press. Many of the stories are still popular. Some have been made into plays and television programmes. In Scotland, many people continued to speak Gaelic and the Scots language also developed. A number of poets began to write in the Scots language.

One example is John Barbour, who wrote The Bruce about the Battle of Bannockburn. The Middle Ages also saw a change in the type of buildings in Britain. Castles were built in many places in Britain and Ireland, partly for defence. Today many are in ruins, although some, such as Windsor and Edinburgh, are still in use. Great cathedrals – for example, Lincoln Cathedral – were also built, and many of these are still used for worship. Several of the cathedrals had windows of stained glass, telling stories about the Bible and Christian saints. The glass in York Minster is a famous example. During this period, England was an important trading nation. English wool became a very important export. People came to England from abroad to trade and also to work. Many had special skills, such as weavers from France, engineers from Germany, glass manufacturers from Italy and canal builders from Holland.

The Wars of The Roses

In 1455, a civil war was begun to decide who should be king of England. It was fought between the supporters of two families: the House of Lancaster and the House of York. This war was called the Wars of the Roses, because the symbol of Lancaster was a red rose and the symbol of York was a white rose. The war ended with the Battle of Bosworth Field in 1485. King Richard III of the House of York was killed in the battle and Henry Tudor, the leader of the House of Lancaster, became King Henry VII. Henry then married King Richard's niece, Elizabeth of York, and united the two families. Henry was the first king of the House of Tudor. The symbol of the House of Tudor was a red rose with a white rose inside it as a sign that the Houses of York and Lancaster were now allies.

Check that you understand

- The wars that took place in the Middle Ages
- How Parliament began to develop
- The way that land ownership worked
- The effects of the Black Death
- The development of English language and culture
- The Wars of the Roses the founding of the House of Tudor

The Tudors and Stuarts

After his victory in the Wars of the Roses, Henry VII wanted to make sure that England remained peaceful and that his position as king was secure. He deliberately strengthened the central administration of England and reduced the power of the nobles. He was thrifty and built up the monarchy's financial reserves. When he died, his son Henry VIII continued the policy of centralising power. Henry VIII was most famous for breaking away from the Church of Rome and marrying six times.

The six wives of Henry VIII

Catherine of Aragon – Catherine was a Spanish princess. She and Henry had a number of children but only one, Mary, survived. When Catherine was too old to give him another child, Henry decided to divorce her, hoping that another wife would give him a son to be his heir.

Anne Boleyn – Anne Boleyn was English. She and Henry had one daughter, Elizabeth. Anne was unpopular in the country and was accused of taking lovers. She was executed at the tower of London.

Jane Seymour – Henry married Jane after Anne's execution. She gave Henry the son he wanted, Edward, but she died shortly after his birth.

Anne of Cleves – Anne was a German princess. Henry married her for political reasons but divorced her soon after.

Catherine Howard – Catherine was a cousin of Anne Boleyn. She was also accused of taking lovers and executed.

Catherine Parr – Catherine was a widow who married Henry later in his life. She survived him and married again but died soon after.

To divorce his first wife, Henry needed the approval of the Pope. When the Pope refused, Henry established the church of England. In this new church, the king, not the Pope, would have the power to appoint bishops and order how people should worship. At the same time the Reformation was happening across Europe. This was a movement against the authority of the Pope and the ideas and practices of the Roman Catholic Church. The Protestants formed their own churches. They read the Bible in their own languages instead of Latin; they did not pray to saints or at shrines; and they believed that a person's own relationship with God was more important than submitting to the authority of the Church.

Protestant ideas gradually gained strength in England, Wales and Scotland during the 16th century. In Ireland, however, attempts by the English to impose Protestantism (alongside efforts to introduce the English system of laws about the inheritance of land) led to rebellion from the Irish chieftains, and much brutal fighting followed. During the reign of Henry VIII, Wales became formally united with England by the Act for the Government of Wales. The Welsh sent representatives to the House of Commons and the Welsh legal system was reformed. Henry VIII was succeeded by his son Edward VI, who was strongly Protestant. During his reign, the Book of Common Prayer was written to be used in the Church of England. A version of this book is still used in some churches today. Edward died at the age of 15 after ruling for just over six years, and his half-sister Mary became queen. Mary was a devout Catholic and persecuted Protestants (for this reason, she became known as 'Bloody Mary'). Mary also died after a short reign and the next monarch was her half-sister, Elizabeth, the daughter of Henry VIII and Anne Boleyn.

Queen Elizabeth I

Queen Elizabeth I was a Protestant. She re-established the Church of England as the official Church of England. Everyone had to attend their local church and there were laws about the type of religious services and the prayers which could be said, but Elizabeth did not ask about people's real beliefs. She succeeded in finding a balance between the views of the Catholics and the more extreme Protestants. In this way, she avoided any serious religious conflict within England. Elizabeth became one of the most popular monarchs in English history, particularly after 1588, when the English defeated the Spanish Armada (a large fleet of ships), which had been sent by Spain to conquer England and restore Catholicism.

The Reformation in Scotland and Mary, Queen of Scots

Scotland had also been strongly influenced by Protestant ideas. In 1560, the predominantly Protestant Scottish Parliament abolished the authority of the Pope in Scotland and Roman Catholic religious services became illegal. A Protestant Church of Scotland with an elected leadership was established but, unlike in England, this was not a state Church.

The queen of Scotland, Mary Stuart (often now called 'Mary, Queen of Scots') was a Catholic. She was only a week old when her father died and she became queen. Much of her childhood was spent in France. When she returned to Scotland, she was the centre of a power struggle between different groups. When her husband was murdered, Mary was suspected of involvement and fled to England. She gave her throne to her Protestant son, James VI of Scotland.

Mary was Elizabeth I's cousin and hoped that Elizabeth might help her, but Elizabeth suspected Mary of wanting to take over the English throne, and kept her prisoner for 20 years. Mary was eventually executed, accused of plotting against Elizabeth I.

Exploration, Poetry and Drama

The Elizabethan period in England was a time of growing patriotism: a feeling of pride in being English, English explorers sought new trade routes and tried to expand British trade into the Spanish colonies in the Americas. Sir Francis Drake, one of the commanders in the defeat of the Spanish Armada, was one of the founders of England's naval tradition. His ship, the Golden Hind, was one of the first to sail right around ('circumnavigate') the world. In Elizabeth I's time, English settlers first began to colonise the eastern coast of America. This colonisation, particularly by people who disagreed with the religious views of the next two kings, greatly increased in the next century.

The Elizabethan period is also remembered for the richness of its poetry and drama, especially the plays and poems of William Shakespeare.

James VI and I

Elizabeth I never married and so had no children of her own to inherit her throne. When she died in 1603 her heir was her cousin James VI of Scotland. He became King James I of England, Wales and Ireland but Scotland remained a separate country.

The King James Bible

One achievement of King James' reign was a new translation of the Bible into English. This translation is known as the 'King James Version' or the 'Authorised Version'. It was not the first English Bible but is a version which continues to be used in many Protestant churches today.

Ireland

During this period, Ireland was an almost completely Catholic country. Henry VII and Henry VIII had extended English control outside the Pale and had established English authority over the whole country. Henry VIII took the title 'King of Ireland'. English laws were introduced and local leaders were expected to follow the instructions of the Lord Lieutenants in Dublin. During the reigns of Elizabeth I and James I, many people in Ireland opposed rule by the Protestant government in England. There were a number of rebellions. The English government encouraged Scottish and English Protestants to settle in Ulster, the northern province of Ireland, taking over the land from Catholic landholders. These settlements were known as plantations. Many of the new settlers came from south-west Scotland and other land was given to companies based in London. James later organised similar plantations in several other parts of Ireland. This had serious longterm consequence for the history of England, Scotland and Ireland.

The Rise of Parliament

Elizabeth I was very skilled at managing Parliament. During her reign, she was successful in balancing her wishes and views against those of the House of Lords and those of the House of Commons, which was increasingly Protestant in its views. James I and his son Charles I were less skilled politically. Both believed in the 'Divine Right of Kings': the idea that the king was directly appointed by God to rule. They thought that the king should be able to act without having to seek approval from Parliament. When Charles I inherited the thrones of England, Wales, Ireland and Scotland, he tried to rule in line with this principle. When he could not get Parliament to agree with his religious and foreign policies, he tried to rule without the Parliament at all. For 11 years, he found ways in which to raise money without Parliament's approval but eventually trouble in Scotland meant that he had to recall Parliament.

The Beginning of the English Civil War

Charles I wanted the worship of the Church of England to include more ceremony and introduced a revise Prayer Book. He tried to impose this Prayer Book on the Presbyterian Church in Scotland and this led to serious unrest. A Scottish army was formed and Charles could not find the money he needed for his own army without the help of Parliament. In 1640, he recalled Parliament to ask it for funds. Many in Parliament were Puritans, a group of Protestants who advocated strict and simple religious doctrine and worship. They did not agree with the king's religious views and disliked his reforms of the Church of England. Parliament refused to give the king the money he asked for, even after the Scottish army invaded England.

Another rebellion began in Ireland because the Roman Catholics in Ireland were afraid of the growing power of the Puritans. Parliament took this opportunity to demand control of the English army – a change that would have transferred substantial power from the king to Parliament. In response, Charles I entered the House of Commons and tried to arrest five parliamentary leaders, but they had been warned and were not there. (No monarch has set foot in the Commons since.) Civil war between the king and Parliament could not now be avoided and began in 1642. The country spilt into those who supported the king (the Cavaliers) and those who supported Parliament (the Roundheads).

Oliver Cromwell & The English Republic

The King's army was defeated at the Battles of Marston Moor and Naseby. By 1646, it was clear that the Parliament had won the war. Charles was held prisoner by the parliamentary army. He was still unwilling to reach any agreement with the Parliament and in 1649 he was executed. England declared itself a republic, called the Commonwealth. It no longer had a monarch. For a time, it was not totally clear how the country would be governed. For now, the army was in control. One of its generals, Oliver Cromwell, was sent to Ireland, where the revolt which had begun in 1641 still continued and where there was still a Royalist army. Cromwell was successful in establishing the authority of the English Parliament but did this with such violence that even today Cromwell remains a controversial figure in Ireland. The Scots had not agreed to the execution of Charles I and declared his son Charles II to be king. He was crowned king of Scotland and led a Scottish army into England. Cromwell defeated this army in the Battles of Dunbar and Worcester. Charles II escaped from Worcester, famously hiding in an oak tree on one occasion, and eventually fled to Europe. Parliament now controlled Scotland as well as England and Wales. After his campaign in Ireland and victory over Charles II at Worcester, Cromwell was recognised as the leader of the new republic. He was given the title of Lord Protector and ruled until his death in 1658. When Cromwell died, his son, Richard, became Lord Protector in his place but was not able to control the army or the government. Although Britain had been a republic for 11 years, without Oliver Cromwell there was no clear leader or system of government. Many people in the country wanted stability. People began to talk about the need for a king.

The Restoration

In May 1660, Parliament invited Charles II to come back from exile in The Netherlands. He was crowned King Charles II of England, Wales, Scotland and Ireland. Charles II made it clear that he had 'no wish to go on his travels again'. He understood that he could not always do as he wished but would sometimes need to reach agreement with the Parliament. Generally, Parliament supported his policies. The Church of England again became the established official Church. Both Roman Catholics and Puritans were kept out of power. During Charles II's reign, in 1665, there was a major outbreak of plague in London. Thousands of people died, especially in poorer areas. The following year, a great fire destroyed much of the city, including many churches and St Paul's Cathedral. London was rebuilt with a new St Paul's, which was designed by a famous architect, Sir Christopher Wren. Samuel Pepys wrote about these events in a diary which was later published and is still read today.

The Habeas Corpus Act became law in 1679. This was a very important piece of legislation which remains relevant today. Habeas corpus is Latin for 'you must present the person in court'. The Act guaranteed that no one could be held prisoner unlawfully. Every prisoner has a right to a court hearing. Charles II was interested in science. During his reign, the Royal Society was formed to promote 'natural knowledge'. This is the oldest surviving scientific society in the world. Among its early members were Sir Edmund Halley who successfully predicted the return of the comet now called Halley's Comet, and Sir Isaac Newton.

Isaac Newton (1643-1727)

Born in Lincolnshire, eastern England, Isaac Newton first became interested in science when he studied at Cambridge University. He became an important figure in the field. His most famous published work was Philosophiae Naturalis Principia Mathematica ('Mathematical Principle of Natural Philosophy'), which showed how gravity applied to the whole universe. Newton also discovered that white light is made up of the colours of the rainbow. Many of his discoveries are still important for modern science.

A Catholic King

Charles II had no legitimate children. He died in 1685 and his brother, James, who was a Roman Catholic, became King James II in England, Wales and Ireland and King James VII of Scotland. James favoured Roman Catholics and allowed them to be army officers, which an Act of Parliament had forbidden. He did not seek to reach agreements with Parliament and arrested some of the bishops of the Church of England. People in England worried that James wanted to make England a Catholic country once more. However, his heirs were his two daughters, who were both firmly Protestant, and people thought that this meant there would soon be a Protestant monarch again. Then James's wife had a son. Suddenly, it seemed likely that the next monarch would not be a Protestant after all.

The Glorious Revolution

James II's elder daughter, Mary, was married to her cousin William of Orange, the Protestant ruler of the Netherlands. In 1688, important Protestants in England asked William to invade England and proclaim himself king. When William reached England, there was no resistance. James fled to France and William took over the throne, becoming William III in England, Wales and Ireland, and William II of Scotland. William ruled jointly with Mary. This event was later called the 'Glorious Revolution' because there was no fighting in England and because it guaranteed the power of Parliament, ending the threat of monarch ruling on his or her own as he or she wished. James II wanted to regain the throne and invaded Ireland with the help of a French army. William defeated James II at the Battle of the Boyne in Ireland in 1690, an event which is still celebrated by some in Northern Ireland today. William re-conquered Ireland and James fled back to France. Many restrictions were placed on the Roman Catholic Church in Ireland and Irish Catholics were unable to take part in the government. There was also support for James in Scotland. An attempt at an armed rebellion in support of James was quickly defeated at Killiecrankie. All Scottish clans were required formally to accept William as king by taking an oath. The MacDonalds of Glencoe were late in taking an oath. The memory of this massacre meant some Scots distrusted the new government. Some continued to believe that James was the rightful king, particularly in Scotland. Some joined him in exile in France; others were secret supporters. James' supporters became known as Jacobites.

Check that you understand

• How and why religion changed during this period
• The importance of poetry and drama in the Elizabethan period
• About the involvement of Britain in Ireland
• The development of Parliament and the only period in history when England was a republic •
Why there was a restoration of the monarchy
• How the Glorious Revolution happened

Constitutional Monarchy – The Bill of Rights

At the coronation of William and Mary, a Declaration of Rights was read. This confirmed that the king would no longer be able to raise taxes and administer justice without agreement from Parliament. The balance of power between monarch and Parliament had now permanently changed.

The Bill of Rights, 1689, confirmed the rights of Parliament and the limits of the king's power. Parliament took control of who could be monarch and declared that the king or queen must be a Protestant. A new Parliament had to be elected at least every three years (later this became seven years and now it is five years). Every year the monarch had to ask Parliament to renew funding for the army and the navy. These changes meant that, to be able to govern effectively, the monarch needed to have advisers, or ministers, who would be able to ensure a majority of votes in the House of Commons and the House of Lords. There were two main groups in Parliament, known as the Whigs and the Tories. (The modern Conservative Party is still sometimes referred to as the Tories.) This was the beginning of party politics. This was also an important time for the development of a free press (newspapers and other publications which are not controlled by the government).

From 1695, newspapers were allowed to operate without a government licence. Increasing numbers of newspapers began to be published. The laws passed after the Glorious Revolution are the beginning of what is called 'constitutional monarchy'. The monarch remained very important but was no longer able to insist on particular policies or actions if Parliament did not agree. After William III, the ministers gradually became more important than the monarch but this was not a democracy in the modern sense. The number of people who had the right to vote for members of Parliament was still very small. Only men who owned property of a certain value were able to vote. No women at all had the vote. Some constituencies were controlled by a single wealthy family. They were called the 'pocket boroughs'. Other constituencies had hardly any voters and were called 'rotten boroughs'.

A Growing Population

This was a time when many people left Britain and Ireland to settle in new colonies in America and elsewhere, but others came to live in Britain. The first Jews to come to Britain since the Middle Ages settled in London in 1656. Between 1680 and 1720 many refugees called Huguenots came from France. They were Protestants and had been persecuted for their religion. Many were educated and skilled and worked as scientists, in banking, or in weaving or other crafts.

'The Act' or Treaty of Union in Scotland

William and Mary's successor, Queen Anne, had no surviving children. This created uncertainty over the succession in England, Wales and Ireland and in Scotland. The Act of Union, known as the Treaty of Union in Scotland, was therefore agreed in 1707, creating the Kingdom of Great Britain. Although Scotland was no longer an independent country, it kept its own legal and education systems and Presbyterian Church.

The Prime Minister

When Queen Anne died in 1714, Parliament chose a German, George I, to be the next king, because he was Anne's nearest Protestant relative. An attempt by Scottish Jacobites to put James II's son on the throne instead was quickly defeated. George I did not speak very good English and this increased his need to rely on his ministers. The most important minister in Parliament became known as the Prime Minister. The first man to be called this was Sir Robert Walpole, who was Prime Minister from 1721 to 1742.

The Rebellion of the Clans

In 1745 there was another attempt to put a Stuart king back on the throne in place of George I's son, George II. Charles Edward Stuart (Bonnie Prince Charlie), the grandson of James II, landed in Scotland. He was supported by clansmen from the Scottish highlands and raised an army.

Charles initially had some successes but was defeated by George II's army at the Battle of Culloden in 1746. Charles escaped back to Europe. The clans lost a lot of their power and influence after Culloden.

Chieftains became landlords if they had the favour of the English king, and clansmen became tenants who had to pay for the land they used. A process began which became known as the 'Highland Clearances'. Many Scottish landlords destroyed individual small farms (known as 'crofts') to make space for large flocks of sheep and cattle. Evictions became very common in the early 19th century. Many Scottish people left for North America at this time.

Robert Burns (1759-96)

Known in Scotland as 'The Bard', Robert Burns was a Scottish poet. He wrote in the Scots language, English with some Scottish words and standard English. He also revised a lot of the traditional folk songs by changing or adding lyrics. Burns' best-known work is probably the song Auld Lang Syne, which is sung by people in the UK and other countries when they are celebrating the New Year (or Hogmanay as it is called in Scotland).

The Enlightenment

During the 18th century, new ideas about politics, philosophy and science were developed. This is often called 'the Enlightenment'. Many of the great thinkers of the Enlightenment were Scottish. Adam Smith developed ideas about economics which are still referred to today. David Hume's ideas about human nature continue to influence philosophers. Scientific discoveries, such as James Watt's work on steam power, helped the progress of the Industrial Revolution. One of the most important principles of the Enlightenment was that everyone should have the right to their own political and religious beliefs and that the state should not try to dictate to them. This continues to be an important principle in the UK today.

The Industrial Revolution

Before the 18th century, agriculture was the biggest source of employment in Britain. There were many cottage industries, where people worked from home to produce goods such as cloth and lace. The Industrial Revolution was the rapid development of industry in Britain in the 18th and 19th centuries. Britain was the first country to industrialise on a large scale. It happened because of the development of machinery and the use of steam power. Agriculture and the manufacturing of goods became mechanised. This made things more efficient and increased production. Coal and other raw materials were needed to power the new factories. Many people moved from the countryside and started working in the mining and manufacturing industries. The development of the Bessemer process for the mass production of steel led to the development of the shipbuilding industry and the railways. Manufacturing jobs became the main source of employment in Britain.

Better transport links were needed to transport raw materials and manufactured goods. Canals were built to link the factories to towns and cities and to the ports, particularly in the new industrial areas in the middle and north of England. Working conditions during the Industrial Revolution were very poor. There were no laws to protect employees, who were often forced to work long hours in dangerous situations. Children also worked and were treated in the same way as adults. Sometimes they were treated even more harshly.

This was also a time of increased colonisation overseas. Captain James Cook mapped the coast of Australia and a few colonies were established there. Britain gained control over Canada, and the East India Company, originally set up to trade, gained control of large parts of India. Colonies began to be established in southern Africa. Britain traded all over the world and began to import more goods. Sugar and tobacco came from North America and the west Indies; textiles, tea and spices came from India and the area that is today called Indonesia. Trading and settlements overseas sometimes brought Britain into conflict with other countries, particularly France, which was expanding and trading in a similar way in many of the same areas of the world.

Richard Arkwright (1732-92)

Born in 1732, Arkwright originally trained and worked as a barber. He was able to dye hair and make wigs. When wigs became less popular, he started to work in textiles. He improved the original carding machine. Carding is the process of preparing fibres for spinning into yarn and fabric. He also developed horse-driven spinning mills that used only one machine. This increased the efficiency of production. Later, he used the steam engine to power machinery. Arkwright is particularly remembered for the efficient and profitable way that he ran his factories.

Sake Dean Mahomet (1759-1851)

Mahomet was born is 1759 and grew up in the Bengal region of India. He served in the Bengal army and came to Britain in 1782. He then moved to Ireland and eloped with an Irish girl called Jane Daly in 1786, returning to England at the turn of the century. In 1810 he opened the Hindoostane Coffee House in George Street, London. It was the first curry house to open in Britain. Mahomet and his wife also introduced 'shampooing', the Indian art of head massage, to Britain.

The Slave Trade

This commercial expansion and prosperity was sustained in part by the booming slave trade.

While slavery was illegal within Britain itself, by the 18th century it was a fully established overseas industry, dominated by Britain and the American colonies. Slaves came primarily from West Africa. Travelling on British ships in horrible conditions, they were taken to America and the Caribbean, where they were made to work on tobacco and sugar plantations. The living and working conditions for slaves were very bad. Many slaves tried to escape and others revolted against their owners in protest at their terrible treatment.

There were, however people in Britain who opposed the slave trade. The first formal anti-slavery groups were set up by the Quakers in the late 1700s, and they petitioned Parliament to ban the practice. William Wilberforce, an evangelical Christian and a member of Parliament, also played an important part in changing the law. Along with other abolitionists (people who supported the abolition of slavery), he succeeded in turning public opinion against the slave trade. In 1807, it became illegal to trade slaves in British ships or from British ports, and in 1833 the Emancipation Act abolished slavery throughout the British Empire. The Royal Navy stopped slave ships from other countries, freed the slaves and punished the slave traders. After 1833, 2 million Indian and Chinese workers were employed to replace the freed slaves. They worked on sugar plantations in the Caribbean, in mines in South

Africa, on railways in East Africa and in the army in Kenya.

The American War of Independence

By the 1760s, there were substantial British colonies in North America. The colonies were wealthy and largely in control of their own affairs. Many of the colonist families had originally gone to North America in order to have religious freedom. They were well educated and interested in ideas of liberty.

The British government wanted to tax the colonies. The colonists saw this as an attack on their freedom and said there should be 'no taxation without representation' in the British Parliament. Parliament tried to compromise by repealing some of the taxes, but relationships between the British government and the colonies continued to worsen. Fighting broke out between the colonists and the British forces. In 1776, 13 American colonies declared their independence, stating that people had a right to establish their own governments. The colonists eventually defeated the British army and Britain recognised the colonies' independence in 1783.

War with France

During the 18th century, Britain fought a number of wars with France. In 1789, there was a revolution in France and the new French government soon declared war on Britain. Napoleon, who became Emperor of France, continued the war. Britain's navy fought against combined French and Spanish fleets, winning the Battle of Trafalgar in 1805. Admiral Nelson was in charge of the British fleet at Trafalgar and was killed in the battle.

Nelson's Column in Trafalgar Square, London, is a monument to him. His ship, HMS Victory, can be visited in Portsmouth. The British army also fought against the French. In 1815, the French Wars ended with the defeat of the Emperor Napoleon by the Duke of Wellington at the Battle of Waterloo. Wellington was known as the Iron Duke and later became Prime Minister.

The Union Flag

Although Ireland has had the same monarch as England and Wales since Henry VIII, it had remained a separate country. In 1801, Ireland became unified with England, Scotland and Wales after the Act of Union of 1800. This created the United Kingdom of Great Britain and Ireland. One symbol of this union between England, Scotland, Wales and Ireland was a new version of the official flag, the Union Flag. This is still used today as the official flag of the UK.

The Union Flag consists of three crosses:

• This cross of St George, patron saint of England, is a red cross on a white ground.
• The cross of St Andrew, patron saint of Scotland, is a diagonal white cross on a blue ground.
• The cross of St Patrick, patron saint of Ireland, is a diagonal red cross on a white ground.

The Victorian Age

In 1837, Queen Victoria became queen of the UK at the age of 18. She reigned until 1901, almost 64 years. At the date of writing (2013) this is the longest reign of any British monarch. Her reign is known as the Victorian Age. It was a time when Britain increased in power and influence abroad. Within the UK, the middle classes became increasingly significant and a number of reformers led moves to improve conditions of life for the poor.

During the Victorian period, the British Empire grew to cover all of India, Australia and large parts of Africa. It became the largest empire the world has ever seen, with an estimated population of more than 400 million people. Many people were encouraged to leave the UK to settle overseas. Between 1853 and 1913, as many as 13 million British citizens left the country. People continued to come to Britain from other parts of the world. For example, between 1870 and 1914, around 120, 000 Russian and Polish Jews came to Britain to escape persecution. Many settled in London's East End and in Manchester and Leeds. People from the Empire, including India and Africa, also came to Britain to live, work and study.

Trade and Industry

Britain continued to be a great trading nation. The government began to promote policies of free trade, abolishing a number of taxes on imported goods. One example of this was the repealing of the Corn Laws in 1846. These had prevented the import of cheap grain. The reforms helped the development of the British industry, because raw materials could now be imported cheaply. Working conditions in factories gradually became better. In 1847, the number of hours that women and children could work was limited by law to 10 hours per day.

Better housing began to be built for workers. Transport links also improved, enabling goods and people to move more easily around the country. Just before Victoria came to the throne, the father and son George and Robert Stephenson pioneered the railway engine and a major expansion of the railways took place in the Victorian period. Railways were built throughout the Empire. There were also great advances in other areas, such as the building of bridges by engineers such as Isambard Kingdom Brunel. British industry led the world in the 19th century. The UK produced more than half of the world's iron, coal and cotton cloth. The UK also became a centre for financial services, including insurance and banking.

In 1851, the Great Exhibition opened in Hyde Park in the Crystal Palace, a huge building made of steel and glass. Exhibits ranged from huge machines to handmade goods. Countries from all over the world showed their goods but most of the objects were made in Britain.

Isambard Kingdom Brunel (1806-59)

Brunel was originally from Portsmouth, England. He was an engineer who built tunnels, bridges, railway lines and ships. He was responsible for constructing the Great Western Railway, which was the first major railway built in Britain. It runs from Paddington Station in London to the south west of England, the West Midlands and Wales. Many of Brunel's bridges are still in use today.

The Crimean War

From 1853 to 1856, Britain fought with Turkey and France against Russia in the Crimean War. It was the first war to be extensively covered by the media through news stories and photographs. The conditions were very poor and many soldiers died from illnesses they caught in the hospitals, rather than from war wounds. Queen Victoria introduced the Victoria Cross medal during this war. It honours acts of valour by soldiers.

Florence Nightingale (1820-1910)

Florence Nightingale was born in Italy to English parents. At the age of 31, she trained as a nurse in Germany. In 1854, she went to Turkey and worked in military hospitals, treating soldiers who were fighting in the Crimean War. She and her fellow nurses improved the conditions in the hospital and reduced the mortality rate. In 1860 she established the Nightingale Training School for nurses at St Thomas' Hospital in London.

The school was the first of its kind and still exists today, as do many of the practices that Florence used. She is often regarded as the founder of modern nursing. Ireland in the 19th century Conditions in Ireland were not as good as in the rest of the UK. Two-thirds of the population still depended on farming to make their living, often on very small plots of land. In the middle of the century the potato crop failed, and Ireland suffered a famine. A million people died from disease and starvation. Another million and a half left Ireland. Some emigrated to the United States and others came to England. By 1861 there were large populations of Irish people in cities such as Liverpool, London, Manchester and Glasgow.

The Irish Nationalist movement had grown strongly through the 19th century. Some, such as the Fenians, favoured complete independence. Others, such as Charles Stuart Parnell, advocated 'Home Rule', in which Ireland would remain in the UK but have its own parliament.

The Right to Vote

As the middle classes in the wealthy industrial towns and cities grew in influence, they began to demand more political power. The Reform Act of 1832 had greatly increased the number of people with the right to vote. The act also abolished the old pocket and rotten boroughs and more parliamentary seats were given to the towns and cities. There was a permanent shift of political power from the countryside to the towns but voting was still based on ownership of the property. This meant that members of the working class were still unable to vote.

A movement began to demand the vote for the working classes and other people without property. Campaigners, called the Chartists, presented petitions to Parliament. At first they seemed to be unsuccessful, but in 1867 there was another Reform Act. This created many more urban seats in

Parliament and reduced the amount of property that people needed to have before they could vote. However, the majority of men still did not have the right to vote and no women could vote. Politicians realised that the increased number of voters meant that they needed to persuade people to vote for them if they were to be sure of being elected to Parliament. The political parties began to create organisations to reach out to ordinary voters. Universal suffrage (the right of every adult, male or female, to vote) followed in the next century. In common with the rest of Europe, women in 19th century Britain had fewer rights than men.

Until 1870, when a woman got married, her earnings, property and money automatically belonged to her husband. Acts of Parliament in 1870 and 1882 gave wives the right to keep their own earnings and property. In the late 19th and early 20th centuries, an increasing number of women campaigned and demonstrated for greater rights and, in particular, the right to vote. They formed the women's suffrage movement and became known as the 'suffragettes'.

Emmeline Pankhurst (1858-1928)

Emmeline Pankhurst was born in Manchester in 1858. She set up the women's Franchise League in 1889, which fought to get the vote in local elections for married women. In 1903 she helped found the Women's Social and Political Union (WSPU). This was the first group whose members were called 'suffragettes'. The group used civil disobedience as part of their protest to gain the vote for women.

They chained themselves to railings, smashed windows and committed arson. Many of the women, including Emmeline, went on a hunger strike. In 1918, women over the age of 30 were given voting rights and the right to stand for Parliament, partly in recognition of the contribution women made to the war effort during the First World War. Shortly before Emmeline's death in 1928, women were given the right to vote at the age of 21, the same as men.

The Future of the Empire

Although the British Empire continued to grow until the 1920s, there was already discussion in the late 19th century about its future direction. Supporters of expansion believed that the Empire benefited Britain through increased trade and commerce. Others thought the Empire had become over-expanded and that the frequent conflicts in many parts of the Empire, such as India's north-west frontier or southern Africa, were a drain on resources. Yet the great majority of British people believed in the Empire as a force for good in the world.

The Boer War of 1899 to 1902 made the discussions about the future of the Empire more urgent. The

British went to war in South Africa with settlers from the Netherlands called the Boers. The Boers fought fiercely and the war went on for over three years. Many died in the fighting and many more from disease.

There was some public sympathy for the Boers and people began to question whether the Empire could continue. As different parts of the Empire developed, they won greater freedom and autonomy from Britain. Eventually, by the second half of the 20th century, there was, for the most part, an orderly transition from Empire to Commonwealth, with countries being granted their independence.

Rudyard Kipling (1865-1936)

Rudyard Kipling was born in India in 1865 and later lived in India, the UK and the USA. He wrote books and poems set in both India and the UK. His poems and novels reflected the idea that the British Empire was a force for good. Kipling was awarded the Nobel Prize in Literature in 1907. His books include the Just So Stories and The Jungle Book, which continue to be popular today. His poem If has often been voted among the UK's favourite poems. It begins with these words: 'If you can keep your head when all about you are losing theirs and blaming it on you; If you can trust yourself when all men doubt you, But make allowance for their doubting too; If you can wait and not be tired by waiting, or being lied about, don't deal in lies, or being hated, don't give way to hating, And yet don't look too good, nor talk too wise' (If, Rudyard Kipling).

Check that you understand

· The change in the balance of power between Parliament and the monarchy
· When and why Scotland joined England and Wales to become Great Britain
· The reasons for a rebellion in Scotland led by Bonnie Prince Charlie
· The ideas of the Enlightenment
· The importance of the Industrial Revolution and development of industry
· The slave trade and when it was abolished
· The growth of the British Empire · How democracy developed during this period

The First World War

The early 20th century was a time of optimism in Britain. The nation, with its expansive Empire, well-admired navy, thriving industry and strong political institutions, was what is now known as a global 'superpower'. It was also a time of social progress. Financial help for the unemployed, old-age pensions and free school meals were just a few of the important measures introduced. Various laws were passed to improve safety in the workplace; town planning rules were tightened to prevent the further development of slums; and better support was given to mothers and their children after divorce or separation.

Local government became more democratic and a salary for members of Parliament (MPs) was introduced for the first time, making it easier for more people to take part in public life.

This era of optimism and progress was cut short when war broke out between several European nations. On 28 June 1914, Archduke Franz Ferdinand of Austria was assassinated. This set off a chain of events leading to the First World War (1914-18). But while the assassination provided the trigger for war, other factors – such as a growing sense of nationalism in many European states; increasing militarism; imperialism; and the division of the major European powers into two camps – all set the conditions for war.

The conflict was centred in Europe, but it was a global war involving nations from around the world. Britain was part of the Allied Powers, which included (amongst others) France, Russia, Japan, Belgium, Serbia – and later, Greece, Italy, Romania and the United States.

The whole of the British Empire was involved in the conflict – for example, more than a million Indians fought on behalf of Britain in lots of different countries, and around 40, 000 were killed. Men from the West Indies, Africa, Australia, New Zealand and Canada also fought with the British.

The Allies fought against the Central Powers – mainly Germany, the Austro-Hungarian Empire, the Ottoman Empire and later Bulgaria. Millions of people were killed or wounded, with more than 2 million British casualties. One battle, the British attack of the Somme in July 1916, resulted in about 60,000 British casualties on the first day alone.

The First World War ended at 11.00 am on 11th November 1918 with victory for Britain and its allies.

The Partition of Ireland

In 1913, the British government promised 'Home Rule' for Ireland. The proposal was to have a self-governing Ireland with its own parliament but still part of the UK. A Home Rule Bill was introduced in Parliament. It was opposed by the Protestants in the north of Ireland, who threatened to resist Home Rule by force. The outbreak of the First World War led the British government to postpone any changes in Ireland. Irish Nationalists were not willing to wait and in 1916 there was an uprising (the Easter Rising) against the British in Dublin.

The leaders of the uprising were executed under military law. A guerrilla war against the British army and the police in Ireland followed. In 1921 a peace treaty was signed and in 1922 Ireland became two countries. The six countries in the north which were mainly Protestant remained part of the UK under the name Northern Ireland. The rest of Ireland became the Irish Free State. It had its own government and became a republic in 1949. There were people in both parts of Ireland who disagree with the split between the North and the South. They still wanted Ireland to be one independent country. Years of disagreement led to a terror campaign in Northern Ireland and elsewhere.

The conflict between those wishing for full Irish independence and those wishing to remain loyal to the British government is often referred to as 'the Troubles'.

The Inter-War Period

In the 1920s, many people's living conditions got better. There were improvements in public housing and new homes were built in many towns and cities. However, in 1929, the world entered the 'Great Depression' and some parts of the UK suffered mass unemployment. The effects of the depression of the 1930s were felt differently in different parts of the UK.
 The traditional heavy industries such as shipbuilding were badly affected but new industries – including the automobile and aviation industries – developed. As prices generally fell,

those in work had more money to spend. Car ownership doubled from 1 million to 2 million between 1930 and 1939. In addition, many new houses were built. It was also a time of cultural blossoming, with writers such as Graham Greene and Evelyn Waugh prominent. The economist John Maynard Keynes published influential new theories of economics. The BBC started radio broadcasts in 1922 and began the world's first regular television service in 1936.

The Second World War

Adolf Hitler came to power in Germany in 1933. He believed that the conditions imposed on Germany by the Allies after the First World War were unfair; he also wanted to conquer more land for the German people. He set about renegotiating treaties, building up arms, and testing Germany's military strength in nearby countries. The British government tried to avoid another war. However, when Hitler invaded Poland in 1939, Britain and France declared war in order to stop his aggression. The war was initially fought between the Axis powers (fascist Germany and Italy and the Empire of Japan) and the Allies. The main countries on the allied side were the UK, France, Poland, Australia, New Zealand, Canada, and the Union of South Africa. Having occupied Austria and invaded Czechoslovakia, Hitler followed his invasion of Poland by taking control of Belgium and the Netherlands. Then, in 1940, German forces defeated allied troops and advanced through France. At this time of national crisis, Winston Churchill became Prime Minister and Britain's war leader.

As France fell, the British decided to evacuate British and French solders from France in a huge naval operation. Many civilian volunteers in small pleasure and fishing boats from Britain helped the Navy to rescue more than 300,000 men from the beaches around Dunkirk. Although many lives and a lot of equipment were lost, the evacuation was a success and meant that Britain was better able to continue the fight against the Germans.

The evacuation gave rise to the phrase 'the Dunkirk spirit'. From the end of June 1940 until the German invasion of the Soviet Union in June 1941, Britain and the Empire stood almost alone against Nazi Germany. Hitler wanted to invade Britain, but before sending in troops, Germany needed to control the air campaign against Britain, but the British resisted with their fighter planes and eventually won the crucial aerial battle against the Germans, called 'the Battle of Britain', in the summer of 1940. The most important planes used by the Royal Air Force in the Battle of Britain were the Spitfire and the Hurricane – which were designed and built in Britain.

Despite this crucial victory, the German air force was able to continue bombing London and other British cities at night-time. This was called the Blitz.

Coventry was almost totally destroyed and a great deal of damage was done in other cities, especially in the East End of London. Despite the destruction, there was a strong national spirit of resistance in the UK. The phrase 'the Blitz spirit' is still used today to describe Britons pulling together in the face of adversity. At the same time as defending Britain, the British military was fighting the Axis on many other fronts. In Singapore, the Japanese defeated the British and then occupied Burma, threatening India. The United States entered the war when the Japanese bombed its naval base at Pearl Harbor in December 1941.

That same year, Hitler attempted the largest invasion in history by attacking the Soviet Union. It was a fierce conflict, with huge losses on both sides. German forces were ultimately repelled by the Soviets, and the damage they sustained proved to be a pivotal point in the war. The allied forces gradually gained the upper hand, winning significant victories in North Africa and Italy. German losses in the Soviet Union, combined with the support of the Americans, meant that the Allies were eventually strong enough to attack Hitler's forces in Western Europe. On 6 June 1944, allied forces landed in Normandy (this event is often referred to as 'D-Day'). Following victory on the beaches of Normandy, the allied forces pressed on through France and eventually into Germany. The Allies comprehensively defeated Germany in May 1945.

The war against Japan ended in August 1945 when the United States dropped its newly developed atom bombs on the Japanese cities of Hiroshima and Nagasaki. Scientists led by Ernest Rutherford, working at Manchester and then Cambridge University, were the first to 'split the atom' and took part in the Manhattan Project in the United States, which developed the atomic bomb. The war was finally over.

Winston Churchill (1874-1965)

Churchill was the son of a politician and, before becoming a Conservative MP in 1900, was a soldier and journalist. In May 1940 he became Prime Minister. He refused to surrender to the Nazis and was an inspirational leader to the British people in a time of hardship. He lost the General Election in 1945 but returned as Prime Minister in 1951. He was an MP until he stood down at the 1964 General Election. Following his death in 1965, he was given a state funeral. He remains a much admired figure to this day, and in 2002 was voted the greatest Briton of all time by the public. During the War, he made many famous speeches including lines which you may still hear: 'I have nothing to offer but blood, toil, tears and sweat' Churchill's first speech to the House of Commons after he became Prime Minister, 1940 'We shall fight on the beaches, we shall fight on the landing grounds, we shall fight in the fields and in the streets, we shall fight in the hills; we shall never surrender'.

Alexander Fleming (1881-1955)

Born in Scotland, Fleming moved to London as a teenager and later qualified as a doctor. He was researching influenza (the 'flu') in 1928 when he discovered penicillin. This was then further developed into a usable drug by the scientists Howard Florey and Ernst Chain. By the 1940s it was in mass production. Fleming won the Nobel Prize in Medicine in 1945. Penicillin is still used to treat bacterial infections today.

Check that you understand
· What happened during the First World War
· The partition of Ireland and the establishment of the UK as it is today
· The events of the Second World War

The Welfare State

Although the UK had won the war, the country was exhausted economically and the people wanted change. During the war, there had been significant reforms to the educational system and people now looked for wider social reforms. In 1945 the British people elected a Labour government. The new Prime Minister was Clement Attlee, who promised to introduce the welfare state outlined in the Beveridge Report. In 1948, Aneurin (Nye) Bevan, the Minister for Health, led the establishment of the National Health Service (NHS), which guaranteed a minimum standard of health care for all, free at the point of use. A national system of benefits was also introduced to provide 'social security', so that the population would be protected from the 'cradle to the grave'.

The government took into public ownership (nationalised) the railways, coal mines and gas, water and electricity supplies. Another aspect of change was self-government for former colonies. In 1947, independence was granted to nine countries, including India, Pakistan and Ceylon (now Sri Lanka). Other colonies in Africa, the Caribbean and the Pacific achieved independence over the next 20 years.

The UK developed its own atomic bomb and joined the new North Atlantic Treaty Organization (NATO), an alliance of nations set up to resist the perceived threat of invasion by the Soviet Union and it allies. Britain had a Conservative government from 1951 to 1964. The 1950s were a period of economic recovery after the war and increasing prosperity for working people. The Prime Minister of the day, Harold Macmillan, was famous for his 'wind of change' speech about decolonisation and independence for the countries of the Empire.

Clement Attlee (1883-1967)

Clement Attlee was born in London in 1883. His father was a solicitor and, after studying at Oxford University, Attlee became a barrister. He gave this up to do social work in East London and eventually became a Labour MP. He was Winston Churchill's Deputy Prime Minister in the wartime coalition government and became Prime Minister after the Labour Party won the 1945 election. He was Prime Minister from 1945 to 1951 and led the Labour Party for 20 years. Attlee's government undertook the nationalisation of major industries (like coal and steel), created the National Health Service and implemented many of Beveridge's plans for a stronger welfare state. Attlee also introduced measures to improve the conditions of workers.

William Beveridge (1879-1963)

William Beveridge (later Lord Beveridge) was a British economist and reformer. He served briefly as a Liberal MP and was subsequently the leader of the Liberals in the House of Lords but is best known for the 1942 report Social Insurance and Allied Services (known as the Beveridge Report). The report was commissioned by the wartime government in 1941. It recommended that the government should find ways of fighting the five 'Giant Evils' of Want, Disease, Ignorance, Squalor and Idleness and provided the basis of the modern welfare state.

R A Butler (1902-82)

Richard Austen Butler (later Lord Butler) was born in 1902. He became a Conservative MP in 1923 and held several positions before becoming responsible for education in 1941. In this role, he oversaw the introduction of the Education Act 1944 (often called 'The Butler Act'), which introduced free secondary education in England and Wales. The education system has changed significantly since the Act was introduced, but the division between primary and secondary schools that it enforced still remains in most areas of Britain.

Dylan Thomas (1914-53)

Dylan Thomas was a Welsh poet and writer. He often read and performed his work in public, including for the BBC. His most well-known works include the radio play Under Milk Wood, first performed after his death in 1954, and the poem Do Not Go Gentle into That Good Night, which he wrote for his dying father in 1952. He died at the age of 39 in New York. There are several memorials to him in his birthplace, Swansea, including a statue and the Dylan Thomas Centre.

Migration in Post-War Britain

Rebuilding Britain after the Second World War was a huge task. There were labour shortages and the British government encouraged workers from Ireland and other parts of Europe to come to the UK and help with the reconstruction. In 1948, people from the West Indies were also invited to come and work.

During the 1950s, there was still a shortage of labour in the UK. Further immigration was therefore encouraged for economic reasons, and many industries advertised for workers from overseas. For example, centres were set up in the West Indies to recruit people to drive buses. Textile and engineering firms from the north of England and the Midlands sent agents to India and Pakistan to find workers. For about 25 years, people from the West Indies, India, Pakistan and (later) Bangladesh travelled to work and settle in Britain.

Social change in the 1960s

The decade of the 1960s was a period of significant social change. It was known as the 'swinging sixties'. There was growth in British fashion, cinema and popular music. Two well-known pop music groups at the time were The Beatles and The Rolling Stones. People started to become better off and many bought cars and other consumer goods.

It was also a time when social laws were liberalised, for example in relation to divorce and to abortion in England, Wales and Scotland. The position of women in the workplace also improved. It was quite common at the time for employers to ask women to leave their jobs when they got married, but Parliament passed new laws giving women the right to equal pay and made it illegal for employers to discriminate against women because of their gender.

The 1960s was also a time of technological progress. Britain and France developed the world's only supersonic commercial airliner, Concorde. New styles of architecture, including high-rise buildings and the use of concrete and steel, became common. The number of people migrating from the West Indies, India, Pakistan and what is now Bangladesh fell in the late 1960s because the government passed new laws to restrict immigration to Britain. Immigrants were required to have a strong connection to Britain through birth or ancestry. Even so, during the early 1970s, Britain admitted 28,000 people of Indian origin who had been forced to leave Uganda.

Some great British inventions of the 20th century

Britain has given the world some wonderful inventions. Examples from the 20th century include:

The television was developed by Scotsman John Logie Baird (1888-1946) in the 1920s. In 1932 he made the first television broadcast between London and Glasgow.

Radar was developed by Scotsman Sir Robert Watson-Watt (1892-1973), who proposed that enemy aircraft could be detected by radio waves. The first successful radar test took place in 1935. Working with radar led Sir Bernard Lovell (1913-2012) to make new discoveries in astronomy.

The radio telescope he built at Jodrell Bank in Cheshire was for many years the biggest in the world and continues to operate today.

A Turing machine is a theoretical mathematical device invented by Alan Turing (1912-54), a British mathematician, in the 1930s. The theory was influential in the development of computer science and the modern-day computer.

The Scottish physician and researcher John Macleod (1876-1935) was the codiscoverer of insulin, used to treat diabetes.

The structure of the DNA molecule was discovered in 1953 through work at British universities in London and Cambridge. This discovery contributed to many scientific advances, particularly in medicine and fighting crime.

Francis Crick (1916-2004), one of those awarded the Nobel Prize for this discovery, was British. The jet engine was developed in Britain in the 1930s by Sir Frank Whittle (1907-96), a British Royal Air Force engineer officer.

Sir Christopher Cockrell (1910-99), a British inventor, invented the hovercraft in the 1950s. Britain and France developed Concorde, the world's only supersonic passenger aircraft. It first flew in 1969 and began carrying passengers in 1976. Concorde was retired from service in 2003. The Harrier jump jet, an aircraft capable of taking off vertically, was also designed and developed in the UK. In the 1960s,

James Goodfellow (1937-) invented the cash-dispensing ATM (automatic teller machine) or 'cashpoint'. The first of these was put into use by Barclays Bank in Enfield, north London in 1967. IVF (in-vitro fertilisation) therapy for the treatment of infertility was pioneered in Britain by physiologist Sir Robert Edwards (1925-) and gynaecologist

Patrick Steptoe (1913-88). The world's first 'test-tube baby' was born in Oldham, Lancashire in 1978. In 1996, two British scientists, Sir Ian Wilmot (1944-) and Keith Campbell (1954-2012), led a team which was the first to succeed in cloning a mammal, Dolly the sheep. This has led to further research into the possible use of cloning to preserve endangered species and for medical purposes.

Sir Peter Mansfield (1933-), a British scientist, is the co-inventor of the MRI (magnetic resonance imaging) scanner. This enables doctors and researchers to obtain exact and non-invasive images of human internal organs and has revolutionised diagnostic medicine.

The inventor of the World Wide Web, Sir Tim Berners-Lee (1955-), is British. Information was successfully transferred via the web for the first time on 25 December 1990.

Problem in the economy in the 1970s

In the late 1970s, the post-war economic boom came to an end. Prices of goods and raw materials began to rise sharply and the exchange rate between the pound and other currencies was unstable. This caused problems with the 'balance of payments': imports of goods were valued at more than the price paid for exports. Many industries and services were affected by strikes and this caused problems between the trade unions and the government. People began to argue that the unions were too powerful and that their activities were harming the UK.

The 1970s were also a time of serious unrest in Northern Ireland. In 1972, the Northern Ireland Parliament was suspended and Northern Ireland was directly ruled by the UK government. Some 3,000 people lost their lives in the decades after 1969 in the violence of Northern Ireland.

Mary Peters (1939-)

Born in Manchester, Mary Peters moved to Northern Ireland as a child. She was a talented athlete who won an Olympic gold medal in the pentathlon in 1972. After this, she raised money for local athletics and became the team manager for the women's British Olympic team. She continues to promote sport and tourism in Northern Ireland and was made a Dame of the British Empire in 2000 in recognition of her work.

Europe and the Common Market

West Germany, France, Belgium, Italy, Luxembourg and the Netherlands formed the European Economic Community (EEC) in 1957. At first the UK did not wish to join the EEC but it eventually did so in 1973. The UK voted to leave the EU in 2016 and eventually left the EU in 2020.

Conservative government from 1979 to 1997

Margaret Thatcher, Britain's first woman Prime Minister, led the Conservative government from 1979 to 1990. The government made structural changes to the economy through the privatisation of nationalised industries and imposed legal controls on trade union powers. Deregulation saw a great increase in the role of the City of London as an international centre for investments, insurance and other financial services. Traditional industries, such as shipbuilding and coal mining, declined. In 1982, Argentina invaded the Falkland Islands, a British overseas territory in the South Atlantic. A naval taskforce was sent from the UK and military action led to the recovery of the islands. John Major was Prime Minister after Mrs Thatcher, and helped establish the Northern Ireland peace process.

Margaret Thatcher (1925-2013)

Margaret Thatcher was the daughter of a grocer from Grantham in Lincolnshire. She trained as a chemist and lawyer. She was elected as a Conservative MP in 1959 and became a cabinet minister in 1970 as the Secretary of State for Education and Science. In 1975 she was elected as Leader of the Conservative Party and so became Leader of the Opposition. Following the Conservative victory in the General Election in 1979,

Margaret Thatcher became the first woman Prime Minister of the UK. She was the longest-serving Prime Minister of the 20th century, remaining in office until 1990. Margaret Thatcher, the first female Prime Minister of the UK During her premiership, there were a number of important economic reforms within the UK. She worked closely with the United States President, Ronald Reagan, and was one of the first Western leaders to recognise and welcome the changes in the leadership of the Soviet Union which eventually led to the end of the Cold War.

Roald Dahl (1916-90)

Roald Dahl was born in Wales to Norwegian parents. He served in the Royal Air Force during the Second World War. It was during the 1940s that he began to publish books and short stories. He is most well known for his children's books, although he also wrote for adults. His best-known works include Charlie and the Chocolate Factory and George's Marvellous Medicine. Several of his books have been made into films.

Labour government from 1997 to 2010

In 1997 the Labour Party led by Tony Blair was elected. The Blair government introduced a

Scottish Parliament and a Welsh Assembly (see page 129). The Scottish Parliament has substantial powers to legislate. The Welsh Assembly was given fewer legislative powers but considerable control over public services. In Northern Ireland, the Blair government was able to build on the Peace process, resulting in the Good Friday Agreement signed in 1998. The Northern Ireland Assembly was elected in 1999 but suspended in 2002. It was not reinstated until 2007. Most paramilitary groups in Northern Ireland have decommissioned their arms and are inactive. Gordon Brown took over as Prime Minister in 2007.

Conflicts in Afghanistan and Iraq

Throughout the 1990s, Britain played a leading role in coalition forces involved in the liberation of Kuwait, following the Iraqi invasion in 1990, and the conflict in the former Republic of Yugoslavia. Since 2000, British armed forces have been engaged in the global fight against international terrorism and against the proliferation of weapons of mass destruction, including operations in Afghanistan and Iraq. British combat troops left Iraq in 2009. The UK now operates in Afghanistan as part of the United Nations (UN) mandated 50-nation International Security Assistance Force (ISAF) coalition and at the invitation of the Afghan government. ISAF is working to ensure that Afghan territory can never again be used as a safe haven for international terrorism, where groups such as Al

Qa'ida could plan attacks on the international community. As part of this, ISAF is building up the Afghan National Security Forces and is helping to create a secure environment in which governance and development can be extended. International forces are gradually handing over responsibility for security to the Afghans, who will have full security responsibility in all provinces by the end of 2014.

Coalition government 2010 onwards

In May 2010, and for the first time in the UK since February 1974, no political party won an overall majority in the General Election. The Conservative and Liberal Democrat parties formed a coalition and the leader of the Conservative Party, David Cameron, became Prime Minister.

Check that you understand

· The establishment of the welfare state
· How life in Britain changed in the 1960s and 1970s
· British inventions of the 20th century (you do not need to remember dates of births and deaths)
· Events since 1979

Chapter 4 - A Modern, Thriving Society

The UK Today

The UK today is a more diverse society than it was 100 years ago, in both ethnic and religious terms. Post-war immigration means that nearly 10% of the population has a parent or grandparent born outside the UK. The UK continues to be a multinational and multiracial society with a rich and varied culture. This section will tell you about the different parts of the UK and some of the important places. It will also explain some of the UK's traditions and customs and some of the popular activities that take place. The nations of the UK The UK is located in the north west of Europe. The longest distance on the mainland is from John O'Groats on the north coast of Scotland to Land's End in the south-west corner of England. It is about 870 miles (approximately 1,400 kilometres).

Most people live in towns and cities but much of Britain is still countryside. Many people continue to visit the countryside for holidays and for leisure activities such as walking, camping and fishing.

Languages and Dialects

There are many variations in language in the different parts of the UK. The English language has many accents and dialects. In Wales, many people speak Welsh – a completely different language from English – and it is taught in schools and universities. In Scotland, Gaelic (again, a different language) is spoken in some parts of the Highlands and Islands, and in Northern Ireland some people speak Irish Gaelic.

Population

Population growth has been faster in more recent years. Migration into the UK and longer life expectancy have played a part in population growth. The population is very unequally distributed over the four parts of the UK. England more or less consistently makes up 84% of the total population, Wales around 5%, Scotland just over 8%, and Northern Ireland less than 3%. People in the UK are living longer than ever before. This is due to improved living standards and better health care. There are now a record number of people aged 85 and over. This has an impact on the cost of pensions and health care.

Ethnic Diversity

The UK population is ethnically diverse and changing rapidly, especially in large cities such as London. It is not always easy to get an exact picture of the ethnic origin of all the population. There are people in the UK with ethnic origins from all over the world. In surveys, the most common ethnic description chosen is white, which includes people of European, Australian, Canadian, New Zealand and American descent. Other significant groups are those of Asian, black and mixed descent.

An Equal Society

Within the UK, it is a legal requirement that men and women should not be discriminated against because of their gender or because the are, or are not, married. They have equal rights to work, own property, marry and divorce. If they are married, both parents are equally responsible for their children.

Women in Britain today make up about half of the workforce. On average, girls leave school with better qualifications than boys. More women than men study at university. Employment opportunities for women are much greater than they were in the past. Women work in all sectors of the economy, and there are now more women in high-level positions than ever before, including senior mangers in traditionally male-dominated occupations. Alongside this, men now work in more varied jobs than they did in the past. It is no longer expected that women should stay at home and not work. Women often continue to work after having children. In many families today, both partners work and both share responsibility for childcare and household chores.

Check that you understand

· The capital cites of the UK
· What languages other than English are spoken in particular parts of the UK
· How the population of the UK has changed
· That the UK is and equal society and ethnically diverse
· The currency of the UK

Religion

The UK is historically a Christian country. In the 2009 Citizenship Survey, 70% of people identified themselves as Christian. Much smaller proportions identified themselves as Muslim (4%), Hindu (2%), Sikh (1%), Jewish or Buddhist (both less than 0.5%), and 2% of people followed another religion. There are religious buildings for other religions all over the UK. This includes Islamic mosques, Hindu temples, Jewish synagogues, Sikh gurdwaras and Buddhist temples. However, everyone has the legal right to choose their religion, or to choose not to practice a religion. In the Citizenship Survey, 21% of people said that they had no religion.

Christian Churches

In England, there is a constitutional link between Church and state. The official Church of the state is the Church of England (called the Anglican Church in other countries and the Episcopal Church in Scotland and the United States). It is a Protestant Church and has existed since the Reformation in the 1530s. The monarch is the head of the Church of England. The spiritual leader of the Church of England is the Archbishop of Canterbury. The monarch has the right to select the Archbishop and other senior church officials, but usually the choice is made by the Prime Minister and a committee appointed by the Church. Several Church of England bishops sit in the House of Lords.

In Scotland, the national Church is the Church of Scotland, which is a Presbyterian Church. It is governed by ministers and elders. The chairperson of the General Assembly of the Church of Scotland is the Moderator, who is appointed for one year only and often speaks on behalf of that Church. There is no established Church in Wales or Northern Ireland. Other Protestant Christian groups in the UK are Baptists, Methodists, Presbyterians and Quakers. There are also other denominations of Christianity, the biggest of which is Roman Catholic.

Patron Saints' Days

England, Scotland, Wales and Northern Ireland each have a national saint, called a patron saint. Each saint has a special day:

- 1 March: St David's Day, Wales
- 17 March: St Patrick's Day, Northern Ireland
- 23 April: St George's Day, England
- 30 November: St Andrew's Day, Scotland.

Only Scotland and Northern Ireland have their patron saint's day as an official holiday (although in Scotland not all businesses and offices will close). Events are held across Scotland, Northern Ireland and the rest of the country, especially where there are a lot of people of Scottish, Northern Irish and Irish heritage. While the patron saints' days are no longer public holidays in England and Wales, they are still celebrated. Parades and small festivals are held all over the two countries.

Check that you understand

- The different religions that are practised in the UK

- That the Anglican Church, also known as the Church of England, is the Church of the state in England (the 'established Church')

• That other branches of the Christian Church also practise their faith in the UK without being linked to the state

• That other religions are practised in the UK

• About the patron saints

Customs and Traditions

Christmas Day, 25 December, celebrates the birth of Jesus Christ. It is a public holiday. Many Christians go to church on Christmas Eve (24 December) or on Christmas Day itself. Christmas is celebrated in a traditional way. People usually spend the day at home and eat a special meal, which often includes roast turkey, Christmas pudding and mince pies. They give gifts, send cards and decorate their houses. Christmas is a special time for children. Very young children believe that Father Christmas (also known as Santa Claus) brings them presents during the night before Christmas Day. Many people decorate a tree in their home.

Boxing Day is the day after Christmas Day and is a public holiday.

Easter takes place in March or April. It marks the death of Jesus Christ on Good Friday and his rising from the dead on Easter Sunday. Both Good Friday and the following Monday, called Easter Monday, are public holidays. The 40 days before Easter are known as Lent. It is a time when Christians take time to reflect and prepare for Easter. Traditionally, people would fast during this period and today many people will give something up, like a favourite food. The day before Lent starts is called Shrove Tuesday, or Pancake Day. People eat pancakes, which were traditionally made to use up foods such as eggs, fat and milk before fasting. Lent begins on Ash Wednesday. There are church services where Christians are marked with an ash cross on their forehead as a symbol of death and sorrow for sin. Easter is also celebrated by people who are not religious. 'Easter eggs' are chocolate eggs given as presents as a symbol of new life.

Other Religious Festivals

Diwali normally falls in October or November and lasts for five days. It is often called the Festival of Lights. It is celebrated by Hindus and Sikhs. It celebrates the victory of good over evil and the gaining of knowledge. There are different stories about how the festival came about. There is a famous celebration of Diwali in Leicester.

Hannukah is in November or December and is celebrated for eight days. It is to remember the Jews' struggle for religious freedom. On each day of the festival a candle is lit on a stand of eight candles (called a menorah) to remember the story of the festival, where oil that should have lasted only a day did so for eight.

Eid a-Fitr celebrates the end of Ramadan, when Muslims have fasted for a month. They thank Allah for giving them the strength to complete the fast. The date when it takes place changes every year. Muslims attend special services and meals.

Eid ul Adha remembers that the prophet Ibrahim was willing to sacrifice his son when God ordered him to . It reminds Muslims of their own commitment to God. Many Muslims sacrifice an animal to eat during this festival. In Britain this has to be done in a slaughterhouse.

Vaisakhi (also spelled Baisakhi) is a Sikh festival which celebrates the founding of the Sikh community known as the Khalsa. It is celebrated on 14 April each year with parades, dancing and singing.

Other Festivals and Traditions

New Year, 1 January, is a public holiday. People usually celebrate on the night of 31 December (called New Year's Eve). In Scotland, 31 December is called Hogmanay and 2 January is also a public holiday. For some Scottish people, Hogmanay is a bigger holiday than Christmas.

Valentine's Day, 14 February, is when lovers exchange cards and gifts. Sometimes people send anonymous cards to someone they secretly admire.

April Fool's Day, 1 April, is a day when people play jokes on each other until midday. The television and newspapers often have stories that are April Fool jokes.

Mothering Sunday (or Mother's day) is the Sunday three weeks before Easter. Children send cards or buy gifts for their mothers.

Father's Day is the third Sunday in June. Children send cards or buy gifts for their fathers.

Halloween, 31 October, is an ancient festival and has roots in the pagan festival to mark the beginning of winter. Young people will often dress up in frightening costumes to play 'trick or treat'. People give them treats to stop them playing tricks on them. A lot of people carve lanterns out of pumpkins and put a candle inside of them.

Bonfire Night, 5 November, is an occasion when people in Great Britain set off fireworks at home or in special displays. The origin of this celebration was an event in 1605, when a group of Catholics led by Guy Fawkes failed in their plan to kill the Protestant king with a bomb in the Houses of Parliament.

Remembrance Day, 11 November, commemorates those who died fighting for the UK and its allies. Originally it commemorated the dead of the First World War, which ended on 11 November 1918. People wear poppies (the red flower found on the battlefields of the First World War). At 11.00 am there is a two-minute silence and wreaths are laid at the Cenotaph in Whitehall, London.

Bank Holidays

As well as those mentioned previously, there are other public holidays each year called bank holidays, when banks and many other businesses are closed for the day. These are of no religious significance. They are at the beginning of May in late May or early June, and in August. In Northern Ireland, the anniversary of the Battle of the Boyne in July is also a public holiday.

Check that you understand

• The main Christian festivals that are celebrated in the UK
• Other religious festivals that are important in the UK
• Some of the other events that are celebrated in the UK

Sport

Sports of all kinds play an important part in many people's lives. There are several sports that are particularly popular in the UK. Many sporting events take place at major stadiums such as Wembley Stadium in London and the Millennium Stadium in Cardiff. Local governments and private companies provide sports facilities such as swimming pools, tennis courts, football pitches, dry ski slopes and gymnasiums. Many famous sports, including cricket, football, lawn tennis, golf and rugby, began in Britain. The UK has hosted the Olympic games on three occasions: 1908, 1948 and 2012. The main Olympic site for the 2012 Games was in Stratford, East London.

The British team was very successful, across a wide range of Olympic sports, finishing third in the medal table. The Paralympic Games for 2012 were also hosted in London. The Paralympics have their origin in the work of Dr Sir Ludwig Guttman, a German refugee, at the Stoke Mandeville hospital in Buckinghamshire. Dr Guttman developed new methods of treatment for people with spinal injuries and encouraged patients to take part in exercise and sport.

Notable British Sportsmen and Women

Sir Roger Bannister (1929-) was the first man in the world to run a mile in under four minutes, in 1954.

Sir Jackie Stewart (1939-) is a Scottish former racing driver who won the Formula 1 world championship three times.

Bobby Moore (1941-93) captained the English football team that won the World Cup in 1966.

Sir Ian Botham (1955-) captained the English cricket team and holds a number of English Test cricket records, both for batting and for bowling.

Jayne Torvill (1957_) and Christopher Dean (1958-) won gold medals for ice dancing at the Olympic Games in 1984 and are some of Britain's greatest Olympians.

Sir Steve Redgrave (1962-) won gold medals in rowing in five consecutive Olympic Games and is one of Britain's greatest Olympians.

Baroness Tanni Grey-Thompson (1969-) is an athlete who uses a wheelchair and won 16 Paralympic medals, including 11 gold medals, in races over five Paralympic Games. She won the

London Marathon six times and broke a total of 30 world records.

Dame Kelly Holmes (1970_) won two gold medals for running in the 2004 Olympic Games. She has held a number of British and European records.

Dame Ellen MacArthur (1976-) is a yachtswoman and in 2004 became the fastest person to sail around the world singlehanded.

Sir Chris Hoy (1976-) is a Scottish cyclist who has won six gold and one silver Olympic medals. He has also won 11 world championship titles.

David Weir (1979-) is a Paralympian who uses a wheelchair and has won six gold medals over two Paralympic Games. He has also won the London Marathon six times.

Bradley Wiggins (1980-) is a cyclist. In 2012, he became the first Briton to win the Tour de France. He has won seven Olympic Medals, including gold medals in the 2004, 2008 and 2012 Olympic Games.

Mo Farah (1983-) is a British distance runner, born in Somalia. He won gold medals in the 2012 Olympics for the 5,000 and 10,000 metres and is the first Briton to win the Olympic gold medal in the 10,000 metres.

Jessica Ennis (1986-) is an athlete. She won the 2012 Olympic gold medal in the heptathlon, which includes seven different track and field events. She also holds a number of British athletics records.

Andy Murray (1987-) is a Scottish tennis player who in 2012 won the men's singles in the US Open. He is the first British man to win a singles title in a Grand Slam tournament since 1936.

Ellie Simmonds (1994-) is a Paralympian who won gold medals for swimming at the 2008 and 2012 Paralympic Games and holds a number of world records. She was the youngest member of the British team at the 2008 Games.

Cricket

Cricket originated in England and is now played in many countries. Games can last up to five days but still result in a draw! The idiosyncratic nature of the game and its complex laws are said to reflect the best of the British character and sense of fair play. You may come across expressions such as 'rain stopped play', 'batting on a sticky wicket', 'playing a straight bat', 'bowled a googly' or 'it's just not cricket', which have passed into everyday usage. The most famous competition is the Ashes, which is a series of Test matches played between England and Australia.

Football

Football is the UK's most popular sport. It has a long history in the UK and the first professional football clubs were formed in the late 19th century. England, Scotland, Wales and Northern Ireland each have separate leagues in which clubs representing different towns and cities compete. The English Premier League attracts a huge international audience. Many UK teams also compete in competitions such as the UEFA (Union of European Football Associations) Champions League, against other teams from Europe. Most towns and cities have a professional club and people take great pride in supporting their home team. There can be great pride in supporting their home team.

There can be great rivalry between different football clubs and among fans. Each country in the UK also has its own national team that competes with other national teams across the world in tournaments such as the FIFA (Fédération Internationale de Football Association) World Cup and UEFA

European Football Championships. England's only international tournament victory was at the World Cup of 1966, hosted in the UK. Football is also a popular sport to play in many local communities, with people playing amateur games every week in parks all over the UK.

Rugby

Rugby originated in England in the early 19th century and is very popular in the UK today. There are two different types of rugby, which have different rules: union and league. Both have separate leagues and national teams in England , Wales, Scotland and Northern Ireland (who play with the Irish Republic). Teams from all countries compete in a range of competitions. The most famous rugby union competition is the Six Nations Championship between England, Ireland, Scotland, Wales, France and Italy. The Super League is the most well-known rugby league (club) competition.

Horse Racing

There is a very long history of horse racing in Britain, with evidence of events taking place as far back as Roman times. The sport has a long association with royalty. There are racecourses all over the UK. Famous horse-racing events include: Royal Ascot , a five-day race meeting in Berkshire attended by members of the Royal Family; the Grand National at Aintree near Liverpool; and the Scottish Grand National at Ayr. There is a National Horseracing Museum in Newmarket, Suffolk.

Golf

The modern game of golf can be traced back to 15th century Scotland. It is a popular sport played socially as well as professionally. There are public and private golf courses all over the UK. St Andrews in Scotland is known as the home of golf. The open championship is the only 'Major' tournament held outside the United States. It is hosted by a different golf course every year.

Tennis

Modern tennis evolved in England in the late 19th century. The first tennis club was founded in Leamington Spa in 1872. The most famous tournament hosted in Britain is The Wimbledon Championships, which takes place each year at the All England Lawn Tennis and Croquet Club. It is the oldest tennis tournament in the world and the only 'Grand Slam' event played on grass.

Water Sports

Sailing continues to be popular in the UK, reflecting our maritime heritage. A British sailor, Sir Francis Chichester, was the first person to sail singlehanded around the world, in 1966/67. Two years later, Sir Robin KnoxJohnston became the first person to do this without stopping. Many sailing events are held throughout the UK, the most famous of which is at Cowes on the Isle of

Wight. Rowing is also popular, both as a leisure activity and as a competitive sport. There is a popular yearly race on the Thames between Oxford and Cambridge Universities.

Motor Sports

There is a long history of motor sport in the UK, for both cars and motor cycles. Motor-car racing in the UK started in 1902. The UK continues to be a world leader in the development and manufacture of motor-sport technology. A Formula 1 Grand Prix event is held in the UK each year and a number of British Grand Prix drivers have won the Formula 1 World Championship. Recent British winners include Damon Hill, Lewis Hamilton and Jenson Button.

Skiing

Skiing is increasingly popular in the UK. Many people go abroad to ski and there are also dry slopes throughout the UK. Skiing on snow may also be possible during the winter. There are five ski centres in Scotland, as well as Europe's longest dry ski slope near Edinburgh.

Arts and Culture

Music is an important part of British culture, with a rich and varied heritage. It ranges from classical music to modern pop. There are many different venues and musical events that take place across the UK. The Proms is an eight-week summer season of orchestral classical music that takes place in various venues, including the Royal Albert Hall in London. It has been in various venues, including the Royal Albert Hall in London. It has been organised by the British Broadcasting Corporation (BBC) since 1927.

The Last Night of the Proms is the most well-known concert and (along with others in the series) is broadcast on television.

Classical music has been popular in the UK for centuries. Henry Purcell (1659-95) was the organist at Westminster Abbey. He wrote church music, operas and other pieces, and developed a British style distinct from that elsewhere in Europe. He continues to be influential on British composers.

The German-born composer George Frederick Handel (1685-1759) spent many years in the UK and became a British citizen in 1727. He wrote the Water Music for King George I and Music for the Royal Fireworks for his son, George II. Both these pieces continue to be very popular. Handel also wrote an oratorio, Messiah, which is sung regularly by choirs, often at Easter time.

More recently, important composers include Gustav Holst (1874-1934), whose work includes The Planets, a suite of pieces themed around the planets and the solar system. He adapted Jupiter, part of the Planets suite, as the tune for I owe to thee my country, a popular hymn in British churches.

Sir Edward Elgar (1857-1934) was born in Worcester, England. His bestknown work is probably the Pomp and Circumstance Marches. March No1 (Land of Hope and Glory) is usually played at the Last Night of the Proms at the Royal Albert Hall.

Ralph Vaughan Williams (1872-1958) wrote music for orchestras and choirs. He was strongly influenced by traditional English folk music.

Sir William Walton (1902-83) wrote a wide range of music, from film scores to opera. He wrote marches for the coronations of King George VI and Queen Elizabeth II but his best-known works are probably Façade, which became a ballet, and Balthazar's Feast, which is intended to be sung by a large choir.

Benjamin Britten (1913-76) is best known for his operas, which include Peter Grimes and Billy Budd. He also wrote A Young Person's Guide to the Orchestra, which is based on a piece of music by Purcell and introduces the listener to the various different sections of an orchestra. He founded the Aldeburgh festival in Suffolk, which continues to be a popular music event of international importance.

Other types of popular music, including folk music, jazz, pop and rock music, have flourished in Britain since the 20th century. Britain has had an impact on popular music around the world, due to the wide use of the English language, the UK's cultural links with many countries, and British capacity for invention and innovation. Since the 1960s, British pop music has made one of the most important cultural contributions to life in the UK. Bands including The Beatles and The Rolling Stones continue to have an influence on music both here and abroad. British pop music has continued to innovate – for example, the Punk movement of the late 1970s, and the trend towards boy and girl bands in the 1990s.

There are many large venues that host music events throughout the year, such as: Wembley Stadium; The O2 in Greenwich, south-east London; and the Scottish Exhibition and Conference Centre (SECC) in Glasgow. Festival season takes place across the UK every summer, with major events in various locations. Famous festivals include Glastonbury, the Isle of Wight Festival and the V Festival. Many bands and solo artists, both well-known and up-and-coming, perform at these events.

The National Eisteddfod of Wales is an annual cultural festival which includes music, dance, art and original performances largely in Welsh. It includes a number of important competitions for Welsh poetry.

The Mercury Music Prize is awarded each September for the best album from the UK and Ireland. The Brit Awards is an annual event that gives awards in a range of categories, such as best British group and best British solo artist.

Theatre

There are theatres in most towns and cities throughout the UK, ranging from the large to the small. They are an important part of local communities and often show both professional and amateur productions. London's west end, also known as 'Theatreland', is particularly well known. The Mousetrap, a murder-mystery play by Dame Agatha Christie, has been running in the west end since 1952 and has had the longest initial run of any show in history. There is also a strong tradition of musical theatre in the UK.

In the 19th century, Gilbert and Sullivan wrote comic operas, often making fun of popular culture and politics. These operas include HMS Pinafore, The Pirates of Penzance and The Mikado. Gilbert and Sullivan's work is still often staged by professional and amateur groups. More recently, Andrew Lloyd Webber has written the music for shows which have been popular throughout the world, including, in collaboration with Tim Rice,

Jesus Christ Superstar and Evita, and also Cats and The Phantom of the Opera.

One British tradition is the pantomime. Many theatres produce a pantomime at Christmas time. They are based on fairy stories and are light-hearted plays with music and comedy, enjoyed by family audiences. One of the traditional characters is the Dame, a woman played by a man. There is often also a pantomime horse or cow played by two actors in the same costume. The Edinburgh Festival takes place in Edinburgh, Scotland, every summer. It is a series of different arts and cultural festivals, with the biggest and most well-known being the Edinburgh Festival Fringe ('the Fringe'). The Fringe is a showcase of mainly theatre and comedy performances. It often shows experimental work.

The Laurence Olivier Awards take place annually at different venues in London. There are a variety of categories, including best director, best actor and best actress. The awards are named after the British actor Sir Laurence Olivier, late Lord Olivier, who was best known for his roles in various Shakespeare plays.

Art

During the Middle Ages, most art had a religious theme, particularly wall paintings in churches and illustrations in religious books. Much of this was lost after the Protestant Reformation but wealthy families began to collect other paintings and sculptures.

Many of the painters working in Britain in the 16th and 17th centuries were from abroad-for example, Hans Holbein and Sir Anthony Van Dyck. British artists, particularly those painting portraits and landscapes, became well known from the 18th century onwards. Works by British and international artists are displayed in Galleries across the UK.
Some of the most well-known galleries are The National Gallery, Tate Britain and Tate Modern in London, the National Museum in Cardiff, and the National Gallery of Scotland in Edinburgh.

Notable British artists

Thomas Gainsborough (1727-88) was a portrait painter who often painted people in country or garden scenery.

David Allan (1744-96) was a Scottish painter who was best known for painting portraits. One of his most famous works is called The Origin of Painting.

Joseph Turner (1775-1851) was an influential landscape painter in a modern style. He is considered the artist who raised the profile of landscape painting.

John Constable (1776-1837) was a landscape painter most famous for his works of Dedham Vale on the Suffolk-Essex border in the east of England.

The Pre-Raphaelites were an important group of artists in the second half of the 19th century. They painted detailed pictures on religious or literary themes in bright colours. The group included Holman Hunt, Dante Gabriel Rossetti and Sir John Millais.

Sir John Lavery (1856-1941) was a very successful Northern Irish portrait painter. His work included painting the Royal Family.
Henry Moore (1898-1986) was an English sculptor and artist. He is best known for his large bronze abstract sculptures.

John Petts (1914-91) was a Welsh artist, best known for his engravings and stained glass.

Lucian Freud (1922-2011) was a German-born British artist. He is best known for his portraits.

David Hockney (1937-) was an important contributor to the 'pop art' movement of the 1960s and continues to be influential today.

The Turner Prize was established in 1984 and celebrates contemporary art. It was named after Joseph Turner. Four works are shortlisted every year and shown at Tate Britain before the winner is announced. The Turner Prize is recognised as one of the most prestigious visual art awards in Europe. Previous winners include Damien Hirst and Richard Wright.

Architecture

The architectural heritage of the UK is rich and varied. In the Middle Ages, great cathedrals and churches were built, many of which still stand today. Examples are the cathedrals in Durham, Lincoln, Canterbury and Salisbury.

The White Tower in the Tower of London is an example of a Norman castle keep, built on the orders of William the Conqueror. Gradually, as the countryside became more peaceful and landowners became richer, the houses of the wealthy became more elaborate and great country houses such as Hardwick Hall in Derbyshire were built. British styles of architecture began to evolve. In the 17th century, Inigo Jones took inspiration from classical architecture to design the Queen's House at Greenwich and the Banqueting House in Whitehall in London.

Later in the century, Sir Christopher Wren helped develop a British version of the ornate styles popular in Europe in buildings such as the new St Paul's Cathedral. In the 18th century, simpler designs became popular. The Scottish architect

Robert Adam influenced the development of architecture in the UK, Europe and America. He designed the inside decoration as well as the building itself in great houses such as Dumfries House in Scotland. His ideas influenced architects in cities such as Bath, where the Royal Crescent was built. In the 19th century, the medieval 'gothic' style became popular again. As cities expanded, many great public buildings were built in this style. The Houses of Parliament and St Pancras Station were built at this time, as were the town halls in cities such as Manchester and Sheffield. In the 20th century, Sir Edwin Lutyens had an influence throughout the British Empire. He designed New Delhi to be the seat of government in India. After the First World War, he was responsible for many war memorials throughout the world, including the Cenotaph in Whitehall. The Cenotaph is the site of the annual Remembrance Day service attended by the Queen, politicians and foreign ambassadors.

Modern British architects including Sir Norman Foster and Lord (Richard) Rogers continue to work on major projects throughout the world as well as within the UK.

Alongside the development of architecture, garden design and landscaping have played an important role in the UK. In the 18th century, Lancelot 'Capability' Brown designed the grounds around country houses so that the landscape appeared to be natural, with grass, trees and lakes. He often said that a place had 'capabilities'. Later, Gertrude Jekyll often worked with worked with Edwin Lutyens to design colourful gardens around the houses he designed. Gardens continue to be an important part of homes in the UK. The annual Chelsea Flower Show showcases garden design from Britain and around the world.

Fashion and Design

Britain has produced many great designers, from Thomas Chippendale (who designed furniture in the 18th century) to Clarice Cliff (who designed Art Deco ceramics) to Sir Terence Conran (a 20th-century interior designer). Leading fashion designers of recent years include Mary Quant, Alexander McQueen and Vivienne Westwood.

Literature

The UK has a prestigious literary history and tradition. Several British writers, including the novelist Sir William Golding, the poet Seamus Heaney, and the playwright Harold Pinter, have won the Nobel Prize in Literature. Other authors have become well known in popular fiction. Agatha Christie's detective stories are read all over the world and Ian Fleming's books introduced James Bond. In 2003, The Lord of the Rings by JRR Tolkien was voted the country's best-loved novel. The Man Booker Prize for Fiction is awarded annually for the best fiction novel written by an author from the Commonwealth, Ireland or Zimbabwe. It has been awarded since 1968. Past winners include Ian McEwan, Hilary Mantel and Julian Barnes.

Notable Authors and Writers

Jane Austen (1775-1817) was an English novelist. Her books include Pride and Prejudice and Sense and Sensibility. Her novels are concerned with marriage and family relationships. Many have been made into television programmes or films.

Charles Dickens (1812-70) wrote a number of very famous novels, including Oliver twist and Great Expectations. You will hear references in everyday talk to some of the characters in his books, such as Scrooge (a mean person) or Mr Micawber (always hopeful).

Robert Louis Stevenson (1850-94) wrote books which are still read by adults and children today. His most famous books include Treasure Island, Kidnapped and Dr Jekyll and Mr Hyde.

Thomas Hardy (1840-1928) was an author and poet. His best-known novels focus on rural society and include Far from the Madding Crowd and Jude the Obscure.

Sir Arthur Conan Doyle (1859-1930) was a Scottish doctor and writer. He was best known for his stories about Sherlock Holmes, who was one of the first fictional detectives.

Evelyn Waugh (1903-66) wrote satirical novels, including Decline and Fall and Scoop. He is perhaps best known for Brideshead Revisited.

Sir Kingsley Amis (1922-95) was an English novelist and poet. He wrote more than 20 novels. The most well known is Lucky Jim.

Graham Greene (1904-91) wrote novels often influenced by his religious beliefs, including The Heart of the Matter, The Honorary Consul, Brighton Rock and Our Man in Havana. J K Rowling (1965-) wrote the Harry Potter series of children's books, which have enjoyed huge international success. She now writes fiction for adults as well.

British Poets

British poetry is among the richest in the world. The Anglo-Saxon poem Beowulf tells of its hero's battles against monsters and is still translated into modern English. Poems which survive from the Middle Ages include Chaucer's Canterbury Tales and a poem called Sir Gawain and the Green Knight, about one of the knights at the court of King Arthur.

As well as plays, Shakespeare wrote many sonnets (poems which must be 14 lines long) and some longer poems. As Protestant ideas spread, a number of poets wrote poems inspired by their religious views. One of these was John Milton, who wrote Paradise Lost.

Other poets, including William Wordsworth, were inspired by nature. Sir Walter Scott wrote poems inspired by Scotland and the traditional stories and songs from the area on the borders of Scotland and England. He also wrote novels, many of which were set in Scotland. Poetry was very popular in the 19th century, with poets such as William Blake, John Keats, Lord Byron, Percy Shelley, Alfred Lord Tennyson, and Robert and Elizabeth Browning.

Later, many poets-for example, Wilfred Owen and Siegfried Sassoon – were inspired to write about their experiences in the First World War. More recently, popular poets have included Sir Walter de la Mare, John Masefield, Sir John Betjeman and Ted Hughes. Some of the best-known poets are buried or commemorated in Poet's Corner in Westminster Abbey.

Some famous lines include:

'Oh, to be in England now that April's there And whoever wakes in England sees, some morning, unaware, That the lowest boughs and the brushwood sheaf Round the elm-tree bole are in tiny leaf While the Chaffinch sings on the orchard bough In England – Now!' (Robert Browning, 1812-89 – Home Thoughts from Abroad)

'She walks in beauty, like the night Of cloudless climes and starry skies, All that's best of dark and bright Meet in her aspect and her eyes' (Lord Byron, 1788-1824 – She walks in Beauty)

'I wander'd lonely as a cloud That floats on high o'er vales and hills When all at once I saw a crowd, A host of golden daffodils' (William Wordsworth, 1770-1850 – The Daffodils)

'Tyger! Tyger! Burning bright In the forests of the night, What immortal hand and eye Could frame thy fearful symmetry?' (William Blake, 1757-1827 – The Tyger)

 'What passing-bells for these who die as cattle? Only the monstrous anger of the guns. Only the stuttering rifles' rapid rattle Can patter out their hasty orisons.' (Wilfred Owen, 1893-1918 – Anthem for Doomed Youth)

Check that you understand

· Which sports are particularly popular in the UK
· Some of the major sporting events that take place each year

Leisure

People in the UK spend their leisure time in many different ways.

Gardening

A lot of people have gardens at home and will spend their free time looking after them. Some people rent additional land called 'an allotment', where they grow fruit and vegetables. Gardening and flower shows range from major national exhibitions to small local events. Many towns have garden centres selling plants and gardening equipment. There are famous gardens to visit throughout the UK, including Kew Gardens, Sissinghurst and Hidcote in England, Crathes Castle and Inveraray Castle in Scotland, Bodnant Garden in Wales, and Mount Stewart in Northern Ireland.

The countries that make up the UK all have flowers which are particularly associated with them and which are sometimes worn on national saints' days:

· England – the rose
· Scotland – the thistle
· Wales – the daffodil
· Northern Ireland – the shamrock.

Shopping

There are many different places to go shopping in the UK. Most towns and cities have a central shopping area, which is called the town centre. Undercover shopping centres are also common – these might be in town centres or on the outskirts of a town or city. Most shops in the UK are open seven days a week, although trading hours on Sundays and public holidays are generally reduced. Many towns also have markets on one or more days a week, where stallholders sell a variety of goods.

Cooking and Food

Many people in the UK enjoy cooking. They often invite each other to their homes for dinner. A wide variety of food is eaten in the UK because of the country's rich cultural heritage and diverse population.

Traditional Foods

There are a variety of foods that are traditionally associated with different parts of the UK:

• England: Roast beef, which is served with potatoes, vegetables, Yorkshire puddings (batter that is baked in the oven) and other accompaniments. Fish and chips are also popular.

• Wales: welsh cakes – traditional Welsh snack made from flour, dried fruits and spices, and served either hot or cold.

• Scotland: Haggis – a sheep's stomach stuffed with offal. Suet, onions and oatmeal.

• Northern Ireland: Ulster fry – a fried meal with bacon, eggs, sausage, black pudding, tomatoes, mushrooms, soda bread and potato bread.

British Film Industry

The UK has had a major influence on modern cinema. Films were first shown publicly in the UK in 1896 and film screenings very quickly became popular. From the beginning, British film makers became famous for clever special effects and this continues to be an area of British expertise. From the early days of the cinema, British actors have worked in both UK and USA. Sir Charles (Charlie) Chaplin became famous in silent movies for his tramp character and was one of many British actors to make a career in Hollywood. British studios flourished in the 1930s.

Eminent directors included Sir Alexander Korda and Sir Alfred Hitchcock, who later left for Hollywood and remained an important film director until his death in 1980. During the Second World War, British movies (for example, In Which

We Serve) played an important part in boosting morale. Later, British directors including Sir David Lean and Ridley Scott found great success both in the UK and internationally. The 1950s and 1960s were a high point for British comedies, including Passport to Pimlico, The Ladykilllers and, later, the Carry On Films.

Many of the films now produced in the UK are made by foreign companies, using British expertise. Some of the most commercially successful films of all time, including the two highest-grossing film franchises (Harry Potter and James Bond), have been produced in the UK. Ealing Studios has a claim to being the oldest continuously working film studio facility in the world. Britain continues to be particularly strong in special effects and animation. One example is the work of Nick Park, who has won four Oscars for his animated films, including three for films featuring Wallace and Gromit.

Actors such as Sir Lawrence Olivier, David Niven, Sir Rex Harrison and Richard Burton starred in a wide variety of popular films. British actors continue to be popular and continue to win awards throughout the world. Recent British actors to have won Oscars include Colin Firth, Sir Antony Hopkins, Dame Judi Dench, Kate Winslet and Tilda Swinton. The annual British Academy Film Awards, hosted by the British Academy of Film and Television Arts (BAFTA), are the British equivalent of the Oscars.

Some famous British films

- The 39 Steps (1935), directed by Alfred Hitchcock
- Brief Encounter (1945), directed by David Lean
- The Third Man (1949), directed by Carol Reed
- The Belles of St Trinian's (1954), directed by Frank Launder
- Lawrence of Arabia (1962), directed by David Lean
- Women in Love (1969), directed by Ken Russel
- Don't Look Now (1973), directed by Nicolas Roeg
- Chariots of Fire (1981), directed by Hugh Hudson
- The Killing Fields (1984), directed by Roland Joffé
- Four Weddings and a Funeral (1994), directed by Mike Newell
- Touching the Void (2003), directed by Kevin MacDonald

British Comedy

The traditions of comedy and satire, and the ability to laugh at ourselves, are an important part of the UK character. Medieval kings and rich nobles had jesters who told jokes and made fun of people in the Court. Later, Shakespeare included comic characters in his plays. In the 18th century, political cartoons attacking prominent politicians – and, sometimes, the monarch or other members of the Royal Family – became increasingly popular. In the 19th century, satirical magazines began to be published. The most famous was Punch, which was published for the first time in the 1840s.

Today, political cartoons continue to be published in newspapers, and magazines such as Private Eye continue the tradition of satire. Comedians were a popular feature of British music hall, a form of variety theatre which was very common until television became the leading form of entertainment in the UK. Some of the people who had performed in the music halls in the 1940s and 1950s, such as Morecambe and Wise, became stars of television.

Television comedy developed its own style. Situation comedies, or sitcoms, which often look at family life and relationships in the workplace, remain popular. Satire has also continued to be important, with shows like That Was The Week That Was in the 1960s and Spitting Image in the 1980s and 1990s. In 1969, Monty Python's Flying Circus introduced a new type of progressive comedy. Stand-up comedy, where a solo comedian talks to a live audience, has become popular again in recent years.

Television and Radio

Many different television (TV) channels are available in the UK. Some are free to watch a wide variety of programmes. Popular programmes include regular soap operas such as Coronation Street and EastEnders. In Scotland, some Scotland-specific programmes are shown and there is also a channel with programmes in the Gaelic language.

There is a Welsh-language channel in Wales. There are also programmes specific to Northern Ireland and some programmes broadcast in Irish Gaelic. Everyone in the UK with a TV, computer or other medium which can be used for watching TV must have a television licence. One licence covers all of the equipment in one home, except when people rent different rooms in a shared house and each has a separate tenancy agreement – those people must each buy a separate licence. People over 75 can apply for a free TV licence and blind people can get a 50% discount. You will receive a fine up to £1,000 if you watch TV but do not have a TV licence. The money from TV licences is used to pay for the British Broadcasting Corporation (BBC). This is a public service broadcaster providing television and radio programmes.

The BBC is the largest broadcaster in the world. It is the only wholly state-funded media organisation that is independent of government. Other UK channels are primarily funded through advertisements and subscriptions.

There are also many different radio stations in the UK. Some broadcast nationally and others in certain cities or regions. There are radio stations that play certain types of music and some broadcast in regional languages such as Welsh or

Gaelic. Like television, BBC radio stations are funded by TV licences and other radio stations are funded through advertisements.

Social Networking

Social networking websites such as Facebook and Twitter are a popular way for people to stay in touch with friends, organise social events, and share photos, videos and opinions. Many people use social networking on their mobile phones when out and about.

Pubs and Night Clubs

Public houses (pubs) are an important part of the UK social culture. Many people enjoy meeting friends in the pub. Most communities will have a 'local' pub that is a natural focal point for social activities. Pub quizzes are popular. Pool and darts are traditional pub games. To buy alcohol in a pub or night club you must be 18 or over, but people under that age may be allowed in some pubs with an adult. When they are 16, people can drink wine or beer with a meal in a hotel or restaurant (including eating areas in pubs) as long as they are with someone over 18. Pubs are usually open during the day from 11.00 am (12 noon on Sundays). Night clubs with dancing and music usually open and close later than pubs. The licensee decides the hours that the pub or night club is open.

Betting and Gambling

In the UK, people often enjoy a gamble on sports or other events. There are also casinos in many places. You have to be 18 to go into betting shops or gambling clubs. There is a National Lottery for which draws are made every week. You can enter by buying a ticket or a scratch card. People under 16 are not allowed to participate in the National Lottery.

Pets

A lot of people in the UK have pets such as cats or dogs. They might have them for company or because they enjoy looking after them. It is against the law to treat a pet cruelly or to neglect it. All dogs in public places must wear a collar showing the name and address of the owner. The owner is responsible for keeping the dog under control and for cleaning up after the animal in a public place.

Vaccinations and medical treatment for animals are available from veterinary surgeons (vets). There are charities which may help people who cannot afford to pay a vet.

Places of Interest

The UK has a large network of public footpaths in the countryside. There are also many opportunities for mountain biking, mountaineering and hill walking. There are 15 national parks in England, Wales and Scotland. They are areas of protected countryside that everyone can visit, and where people live, work and look after the landscape. There are many museums in the UK, which range from small community museums to large national and civic collections. Famous landmarks exist in towns, cities and the countryside throughout the UK. Most of them are open to the public to view (generally for a charge).

Many parts of the countryside and places of interest are kept open by the National Trust in England, Wales and Northern Ireland and the National Trust for Scotland. Both are charities that work to preserve important buildings, coastline and countryside in the UK. The National Trust was founded in 1895 by three volunteers. There are now more than 61,000 volunteers helping to keep the organisation running.

UK Landmarks

Big Ben is the nickname for the great bell of the clock at the House of Parliament in London. Many people call the clock Big Ben as well. The clock is over 150 years old and is a popular tourist attraction. The clock is named 'Elizabeth Tower' in honour of Queen Elizabeth II's Diamond Jubilee in 2012.

The Eden Project is located in Cornwall, in the south west of England. Its biomes, which are like giant greenhouses, house plants from all over the world. The Eden Project is also a charity which runs environmental and social projects internationally.

Edinburgh Castle - The castle is a dominant feature of the skyline in Edinburgh, Scotland. It has a long history, dating back to the early Middle Ages. It is looked after by Historic Scotland, a Scottish government agency.
Located on the north-east coast of Northern Ireland, the Giant's Causeway is a land formation of columns made from volcanic lava. It was formed about 50 million years ago. There are many legends about the Causeway and how it was formed.

Loch Lomond and the Trossachs National Park - This national park covers 720 square miles (1,865 square kilometres) in the west of Scotland. Loch Lomond is the largest expanse of fresh water in mainland Britain and probably the best-known part of the park.

The London Eye is situated on the southern bank of the River Thames and is a Ferris wheel that is 443 feet (135 metres) tall. It was originally built as part of the UK's celebration of the new millennium and continues to be an important part of New Year celebrations.

Snowdonia is a national park in North Wales. It covers an area of 838 square miles (2,170 square kilometres). Its most well-known landmark is Snowdon, which is the highest mountain in Wales.

The Tower of London was first built by William the Conqueror after he became king in 1066. Tours are given by the Yeoman Warders, also known as Beefeaters, who tell visitors about the building's history. People can also see the Crown Jewels there.

The Lake District is England's largest national park. It covers 885 square miles (2,292 square kilometres). It is famous for its lakes and mountains and is very popular with climbers, walkers and sailors. The biggest stretch of water is Windermere. In 2007, television viewers voted Wastwater as Britain's favourite view.

Check that you understand

• Some of the ways in which people in the UK spend their leisure time
• The development of British cinema
• What the television licence is and how it funds the BBC
• Some of the places of interest to visit in the UK

Chapter 5 - The UK Government, the Law and Your Role

Chapter contents

· The development of British democracy
· The British constitution
· The government
· The UK and international institutions
· Respecting the law
· Fundamental principles
· Your role in the community

The Development of British Democracy

Democracy is a system of government where the whole adult population gets a say. This might be by direct voting or by choosing representatives to make decisions on their behalf. At the turn of the 19th century, Britain was not a democracy as we know it today. Although there were elections to select members of Parliament (MPs), only a small group of people could vote. They were men who were over 21 years of age and who owned a certain amount of property. The franchise (that is the number of people who had the right to vote) grew over the course of the 19th century and political parties began to involve ordinary men and women as members.

In the 1830s and 1840s, a group called the Chartists campaigned for reform. They wanted six changes:

• for every man to have the vote
• elections every year
• for all regions to be equal in the electoral system
• secret ballots • for any man to be able to stand as an MP
• for MPs to be paid At the time, the campaign was generally seen as failure.

However, by 1918 most of these reforms had been adopted. The voting franchise was also extended to women over 30, and then in 1928 to men and women over 21. In 1969, the voting age was reduced to 18 for men and women.

The British Constitution

A constitution is a set of principles by which a country is governed. It includes all of the institutions that are responsible for running the country and how their power is kept in check. The constitution also includes laws and conventions. The British constitution is not written down in any single document, and therefore it is described as 'unwritten'. This is mainly because the UK, unlike

America or France, has never had a revolution which led permanently to a totally new system of government. Our most important institutions have developed over hundreds of years. Some people believe that there should be a single document, but others believe an unwritten constitution allows for more flexibility and better government.

Constitutional Institutions

In the UK, there are several different parts of government. The main ones are:

• the monarchy
• Parliament (the House of Commons and the House of Lords)
• the Prime Minister
• the cabinet
• the judiciary (courts)
• the police
• the civil service
• local government

In addition, there are devolved governments in Scotland, Wales and Northern Ireland that have the power to legislate on certain issues.

The Monarchy

King Charles III is the head of state of the UK. He is also the monarch or head of state for many countries in the Commonwealth. The UK has a constitutional monarchy. This means that the king or queen does not rule the country but appoints the government, which the people have chosen in a democratic election. The monarch invites the leader of the party with the largest number of MPs or the leader of a coalition between more than one party, to become the Prime Minister. The monarch has regular meetings with the Prime Minister and can advise, warn and encourage, but the decisions on government policies are made by the Prime Minister and cabinet (see the section on 'The government').

The Queen had reigned since her father's death in 1952, and in 2012 she celebrated her Diamond Jubilee (60 years as queen). She was married to Prince Philip, the Duke of Edinburgh. Her eldest son, previously Prince Charles (the Prince of Wales) succeeded Queen Elizabeth II on the 22nd of September 2022 and is the current Monarch.

The King has important ceremonial roles, such as the opening of the new parliamentary session each year. On this occasion the King makes a speech which summarises the government's policies for the year ahead. All Acts of Parliament are made in his name.

The King represents the UK to the rest of the world. He receives foreign ambassadors and high commissioners, entertains visiting heads of state, and makes state visits overseas in support of diplomatic and economic relationships with other counties. The King has an important role in providing stability and continuity. While governments and Prime Ministers change regularly, the King continues as head of state.

The National Anthem

The National Anthem of the UK is 'God Save the King'. It is played at important national occasions and at events attended by the King or the Royal Family.

The first verse is: 'God save our gracious King! Long live our noble King! God save the King! Send him victorious, Happy and glorious, Long to reign over us, God save the King!'

New citizens swear or affirm loyalty to the King as part of the citizenship ceremony.

Oath of allegiance

I (name) swear by Almighty God that on becoming a British citizen, I will be faithful and bear true allegiance to His Majesty King Charles the Third, his Heirs and Successors, according to law.

Affirmation of allegiance

I (name) do solemnly, sincerely and truly declare and affirm that on becoming a British citizen, I will be faithful and bear true allegiance to His Majesty King Charles the Third, his Heirs and Successors, according to law.

System of Government

The system of government in the UK is a parliamentary democracy. The UK is divided into parliamentary constituencies. Voters in each constituency elect their Member of Parliament (MP) in a General Election. All of the elected MPs form the House of Commons. Most MPs belong to a political party, and the party with the majority of MPs forms the government. If one party does not get a majority, two parties can join together to form a coalition.

The House of Commons

The House of Commons is regarded as the more important of the two chambers in Parliament because its members are democratically elected. The Prime Minister and almost all the members of the cabinet are members of the House of Commons (MPs). Each MP represents a parliamentary constituency, which is a small area of the country. MPs have a number of different responsibilities. They:

• Represent everyone in their constituency
• Help to create new laws

- Scrutinize and comment on what the government is doing
- Debate important national issues

The House of Lords

Members of the House of Lords, known as peers, are not elected by the people and do not represent a constituency. The role and membership of the House of Lords has changed over the last 50 years.

Until 1958, all peers were:

- 'hereditary', which means they inherited their title, or
- senior judges, or
- bishops of the Church of England.

Since 1958, the Prime Minister has had the power to nominate peers just for their own lifetime. These are called life peers. They have usually had an important career in politics, business, law or another profession. Life peers are appointed by the monarch on the advice of the Prime Minister. They also include people nominated by the leaders of the other main political parties or by an independent Appointments Commission for non-party peers. Since 1999, hereditary peers have lost the automatic right to attend the House of Lords. They now elect a few of their number to represent them in the House of Lords.

The House of Lords is normally more independent of the government than the House of Commons. It can suggest amendments or propose new laws, which are then discussed by MPs. The House of Lords checks laws that have been passed by the House of Commons to ensure they are fit for purpose. It also holds the government to account to make sure that it is working in the best interests of the people. There are peers who are specialists in particular areas, and their knowledge is useful in making and checking laws. The House of Commons has powers to overrule the House of Lords, but these are not used often.

The Speaker Debates in the House of Commons are chaired by the Speaker. This person is the chief officer of the House of Commons. The Speaker is neutral and does not represent a political party, even though he or she is an MP, represents a constituency and deals with the constituents' problems like any other MP. The Speaker is chosen by other MPs in a secret ballot. The Speaker keeps order during political debates to make sure the rules are followed. This includes making sure the opposition (see the section on 'The government') has a guaranteed amount of time to debate issues which it chooses. The Speaker also represents Parliament on ceremonial occasions.

Elections

MPs are elected at a General Election, which is held at least every five years.

If an MP dies or resigns, there will be a fresh election, called a by-election, in his or her constituency. MPs are elected through a system called 'first past the post'. In each constituency, the candidate who gets the most votes is elected. The government is usually formed by the party that wins the majority of constituencies. If no party wins a majority, two parties may join together to form a coalition.

Check that you understand

• How democracy has developed in the UK
• What a constitution is and how the UK's constitution is different from those of most other countries
• The role of the monarch
• The role of the House of Commons and House of Lords
• What the Speaker does
• How the UK elects MPs

The Prime Minister

The Prime Minister (PM) is the leader of the political party in power. He or she appoints the members of the cabinet (see below) and has control over many important public appointments. The official home of the Prime Minister is 10 Downing Street, in central London, near the Houses of Parliament. He or she also has a country house outside London called Chequers. The Prime Minister can be changed if the MPs in the governing party decide to do so, or if he or she wishes to resign. The Prime Minister usually resigns if his or her party loses a General Election.

The Cabinet

The Prime Minister appoints about 20 senior MPs to become ministers in charge of departments.

These include:
• Chancellor of the Exchequer – responsible for the economy
• Home Secretary – responsible for crime, policing and immigration
• Foreign Secretary - responsible for managing relationships with foreign countries
• Other ministers (called 'Secretaries of State') responsible for subjects such as education, health and defence. These ministers form the cabinet, a committee which usually meets weekly and makes important decisions about government policy. Many of the decisions have to be debated or approved by Parliament.

Each department also has a number of other ministers, called Ministers of State and

Parliamentary Under-Secretaries of State, who take charge of particular areas of the department's work.

The Opposition

The second-largest party in the House of Commons is called the opposition. The leader of the opposition usually becomes Prime Minister if his of her party wins the next General Election. The leader of the opposition leads his or her party in pointing out what they see as the government's failures and weaknesses. One important opportunity to do this is at Prime Minister's Questions, which takes place every week while Parliament is sitting. The leader of the opposition also appoints senior opposition MPs to be 'shadow ministers'. They form the shadow cabinet and their role is to challenge the government and put forward alternative policies.

The Party System

Anyone aged 18 or over can stand for election as an MP but they are unlikely to win unless they have been nominated to represent one of the major political parties. These are the Conservative Party, the Labour Party, the Liberal Democrats, or one of the parties representing Scottish, Welsh or Northern Irish interests. There are a few MPs who do not represent any of the main political parties. They are called 'independents' and usually represent an issue important to their constituency. The main political parties actively look for members of the public to join their debates, contribute to their costs, and help at elections for Parliament or for local government. They have branches in most constituencies and hold policy-making conferences every year. Pressure and lobby groups are organisations which try to influence government policy. They play an important role in politics. Some are representative organisations such as the CBI (Confederation of British Industry), which represents the views of British business. Others campaign on particular topics, such as the environment (for example, Greenpeace) or human rights (for example, Liberty).

The Civil Service

Civil servants support the government in developing and implementing its policies. They also deliver public services. Civil servants are accountable to ministers. They are chosen on merit and are politically neutral – they are not political appointees. People can apply to join the civil service through an application process, like other jobs in the UK. Civil servants are expected to carry out their role with dedication and a commitment to the civil service and its core values. These are: integrity, honesty, objectivity and impartiality (including being politically neutral).

Local Government

Towns, cities and rural areas in the UK are governed by democratically elected councils, often called 'local authorities'. Some areas have both district and county councils, which have different functions. Most large towns and cities have a single local authority.

Local authorities provide a range of services in their areas. They are funded by money from central government and by local taxes. Many local authorities appoint a mayor, who is the ceremonial leader of the council. In some towns, a mayor is elected to be the effective leader of the administration. London has 33 local authorities, with the Greater London Authority and the Mayor of London coordinating policies across the capital. For most local authorities, local elections for councillors are held in May every year. Many candidates stand for council election as members of a political party.

Devolved Administrations

Since 1997, some powers have been devolved from the central government to give people in Wales, Scotland and Northern Ireland more control over matters that directly affect them. There has been a Welsh Assembly and a Scottish Parliament since 1999. There is also a Northern Ireland Assembly, although this has been suspended on a few occasions. Policy and laws governing defence, foreign affairs, immigration, taxation and social security all remain under central UK government control. However, many other public services, such as education, are controlled by the devolved administrations. The devolved administrations each have their own civil service.

The Welsh Government

The Welsh government and National Assembly for Wales are based in Cardiff, the capital city of Wales. The National Assembly has 60 Assembly members (AMs) and elections are held every four years using a form of proportional representation. Members can speak in either Welsh or English, and all of the Assembly's publications are in both languages.

The Assembly has the power to make laws for Wales in 20 areas, including:

• education and training
• health and social services
• economic development
• housing.

Since 2011, the National Assembly for Wales has been able to pass laws on these topics without the agreement of the UK Parliament.

The Scottish Parliament

The Scottish Parliament was formed in 1999. It sits in Edinburgh, the capital city of Scotland. There are 129 members of the Scottish Parliament (MSPs), elected by a form of proportional representation. The Scottish Parliament can pass laws for Scotland of all matters which are not specifically reserved to the UK Parliament.

The matters on which the Scottish Parliament can legislate include:

· Civil and criminal law
· Health
· Education
· Planning
· Additional tax-raising powers

The Northern Ireland Assembly

A Northern Ireland Parliament was established in 1922, when Ireland was divided, but it was abolished in 1972, shortly after the Troubles broke out in 1969. The Northern Ireland Assembly was established soon after the Belfast Agreement (or Good Friday Agreement) in 1998. There is a power-sharing agreement which distributes ministerial offices amongst the main parties. The Assembly has 108 elected members, known as MLAs (members of the Legislative Assembly). They are elected with a form of proportional representation. The Northern Ireland Assembly can make decisions on issues such as:

· education
· agriculture
· the environment
· health
· social services

The UK government has the power to suspend all devolved assemblies. It has used this power several times in Northern Ireland when local political leaders found it difficult to work together.

The Media and Government

Proceedings in Parliament are broadcast on television and published in official reports called Hansard. Written reports can be found in large libraries and at www.parliament.uk. Most people get information about political issues and events from newspapers (often called 'the press'), television, radio and the internet. The UK has a free press. This means that what is written in newspapers is free from government control. Some newspaper owners and editors hold strong political opinions and run campaigns to try to influence government policy and public opinion. By law, radio and television coverage of the political parties must be balanced and so equal time has to be given to rival viewpoints.

Check that you understand

· The role of the Prime Minister, cabinet, opposition and shadow cabinet.
· The role of political parties in the UK system of government
· Who the main political parties are
· What pressure and lobby groups do
· The role of the civil service
· The role of local government
· The powers of the devolved governments in Wales, Scotland and Northern Ireland
· How proceedings in Parliament are recorded
· The role of the media in keeping people informed about political issues

Who Can Vote?

The UK has had a fully democratic voting system since 1928. The present voting age of 18 was set in 1969 and (with a few exceptions) all UK-born and naturalised adult citizens have the right to vote. Adult citizens of the UK, and citizens of the Commonwealth and the Irish Republic who are resident in the UK, can vote in all public elections. Adult citizens of other EU states who are resident in the UK can vote in all elections except General Elections.

The Electoral Register

To be able to vote, you can register by contacting your local council electoral registration office. This is usually based at your local council (in Scotland it may be based elsewhere). If you don't know which local authority you come under, you can find out by visiting www.aboutmyvote.co.uk and entering you postcode. You can also download voter registration forms in English, Welsh and some other languages.

 The electoral register is updated every year in September or October. An electoral registration form is sent to every household and this has to be completed and returned with the names of everyone who is resident in the household and eligible to vote. In Northern Ireland a different system operates. This is called 'individual registration' and all those entitled to vote must complete their own registration form. Once registered, people stay on the register provided their personal details do not change.

For more information see the Electoral Office for Northern Ireland website at www.eoni.org.uk By law, each local authority has to make its electoral register available for anyone to look at, although this has to be supervised. The register is kept at each local electoral registration office (or council office in England and Wales). It is also possible to see the register at some public buildings such as libraries.

Where to Vote

People vote in elections at places called polling stations, or polling places in Scotland. Before the election you will be sent a poll card. This tells you where your polling station or polling place is and when the election will take place. On election day, the polling station or place will be open from 7.00 am until 10.00 pm. When you arrive at the polling station, the staff will ask for your name and address. In Northern Ireland you will also have to show photographic identification.

You will then get your ballot paper, which you take to a polling booth to fill in privately. You should make up your own mind who to vote for. No one has the right to make you vote for a particular candidate.

You should follow the instructions on ballot paper. Once you have completed it, put it in the ballot box. If it is difficult for you to get to a polling station or polling place, you can register for a postal ballot. Your ballot paper will be sent to your home before the election. You then fill it in and post it back. You can choose to do this when you register to vote.

Standing for Office

Most citizens of the UK, the Irish republic or the Commonwealth aged 18 or over can stand for public office. There are some exceptions, including:

• Members of the armed forces
• Civil servants
• People found guilty of certain criminal offences.

Members of the House of Lords may not stand for election to the House of Commons but are eligible for all other public offices.

The UK Parliament

The public can listen to debates in the Palace of Westminster from public galleries in both the House of Commons and the House of Lords. You can write to your local MP in advance to ask for tickets or you can Queue on the day at the public entrance. Entrance is free. Sometimes there are long queues for the House of Commons and people have to wait for at least one or two hours. It is usually easier to get in to the House of Lords.

Check that you understand

• Who is eligible to vote
• How you register to vote
• How to vote
• Who can stand for public office

The UK and International Institutions

The Commonwealth is an association of countries that support each other and work together towards shared goals in democracy and development. Most member states were once part of the British Empire, although a few countries which were not have also joined. The King is the ceremonial head of the Commonwealth, which currently has 54 member states membership is voluntary.

The European Union

The European Union (EU), originally called the European Economic Community (EEC), was set up by six western European countries (Belgium, France, Germany, Italy, Luxembourg and the Netherlands) who signed the Treaty of Rome on 25 March 1957. The UK originally decided not to join this group but it became a member in 1973. The United Kingdom voted to leave the EU in 2016 and officially left the union in 2020. The UK has several agreements with EU, particularly in relation to Northern Ireland which shares a border with the republic of Ireland, an EU member country.

The Council of Europe

The Council of Europe is separate from the EU. It has 47 member countries, including the UK, and is responsible for the protection and promotion of human rights in those countries. It has no power to make laws but draws up conventions and charters, the most well-known of which is the European Convention on Human Rights and Fundamental Freedoms, usually called the European Convention on Human Rights.

The United Nations

The UK is part of the United Nations (UN), an international organization with more than 190 countries as members. The UN was set up after the Second World War and aims to prevent war and promote international peace and security. There are 15 members on the UN Security Council, which recommends action when there are international crises and threats to peace. The UK is one of five permanent members of the Security Council.

The North Atlantic Treaty Organization (NATO)

The UK is also a member of NATO. NATO is a group of European and North American countries that have agreed to help each other if they come under attack. It also aims to maintain peace between all of its members.

Check that you understand

• What the Commonwealth is and its role
• Other international organisations of which the UK is a member

Respecting the Law

One of the most important responsibilities of all residents in the UK is to know and obey the law.

This section will tell you about the legal system in the UK and some of the laws that may affect you. Britain is proud of being a welcoming country, but all residents, regardless of their background, are expected to comply with the law and to understand that some things which may be allowed in other legal systems are not acceptable in the UK. Those who do not respect the law should not expect to be allowed to become permanent residents of the UK. The law is relevant to all areas of life in the UK. You should make sure that you are aware of the laws which affect your everyday life, including both your personal and business affairs.

The Law in the UK

Every person in the UK receives equal treatment under the law. This means that the law applies in the same way to everyone, no matter who they are or where they are from. Laws can be divided into criminal law and civil law:

• Criminal law relates to crimes, which are usually investigated by the police or another authority such as a council, and which are punished by the courts.

• Civil law is used to settle disputes between individuals or groups.

Examples of criminal laws are:

· Carrying a weapon: it is a criminal offence to carry a weapon of any kind, even if it is for self-defence. This includes a gun, a knife or anything that is made or adapted to cause injury.

· Drugs: selling or buying drugs such as heroin, cocaine, ecstasy and cannabis is illegal in the UK.

· Racial crime: it is a criminal offence to cause harassment, alarm or distress to someone because of their religion or ethnic origin.

· Selling tobacco: it is illegal to sell tobacco products (for example, cigarettes, cigars, roll-up tobacco) to anyone under the age of 18.

· Smoking in public places: it is against the law to smoke tobacco products in nearly every enclosed public place in the UK. There are signs displayed to tell you where you cannot smoke.

· Buying alcohol: it is a criminal offence to sell alcohol to anyone who is under 18 or to buy alcohol for people who are under the age of 18.

· Drinking in public: some places have alcohol-free zones where you cannot drink in public. The police can also confiscate alcohol or move young people on from public places. You can be fined or arrested.

This list does not include all crimes. There are many that apply in most countries, such as murder, theft and assault. You can find out more about types of crime in the UK at www.gov.uk

Example of civil laws are:

• Housing law: this includes disputes between landlords and tenants over issues such as repairs and eviction.

• Consumer rights: an example of this is a dispute about faulty goods or services.

• Employment law: these cases include disputes over wages and cases of unfair dismissal or discrimination in the workplace.

• Debt: people might be taken to court if they owe money to someone.

The police and their duties

The job of the police in the UK is to:

• Protect life and property

• Prevent disturbances (also known as keeping the peace)
• Prevent and detect crime.

The police are organised into a number of separate police forces headed by Chief Constables. They are independent of the government. In November

2012, the public elected Police and Crime Commissioners (PCCs) in England and Wales. These are directly elected individuals who are responsible for the delivery of an efficient and effective police force that reflects the needs of their local communities. PCCs set local police priorities and the local policing budget. They also appoint the local Chief Constable.

The police force is a public service that helps and protects everyone, no matter what their background or where they live. Police officers must themselves obey the law. They must not misuse their authority, make a false statement, be rude or abusive, or commit racial discrimination.

If police officers corrupt or misuse their authority they are severely punished. Police officers are supported by the police community support officers (PCSOs). PCSOs have different roles according to the area but usually patrol the streets, work wth the public, and support police officers at crime scenes and major events.

All people in the UK are expected to help the police prevent and detect crimes whenever they can. If you are arrested and taken to a police station, a police officer will tell you the reason for your arrest and you will be able to seek legal advice.

If something goes wrong, the police complaints system tries to put it right. Anyone can make a complaint about the police by going to a police station and writing to the Chief Constable of the police force involved. Complaints can also be made to an independent body: the Independent Police Complaints Commission in England and Wales, the Police Complaints Commissioner for Scotland or the Police Ombudsman for Northern Ireland.

Terrorism and Extremism

The UK faces a range of terrorist threats. The most serious of these is from Al Qa'ida, its affiliates and like-minded organisations. The UK also faces threats from other kind of terrorism, such as Northern Ireland-related terrorism. All terrorist groups try to radicalise and recruit people to their cause. How, where and to what extent they try to do so will vary. Evidence shows that these groups attract very low levels of public support, but people who want to make their home in the UK should be aware of this threat. It is important that all citizens feel safe. This includes feeling safe from all kinds of extremism (vocal or active opposition to fundamental British values), including religious extremism and far-right extremism. If you think someone is trying to persuade you to join an extremist or terrorist cause, you should notify your local police force.

Check that you understand

- The difference between civil and criminal law and some examples of each
- The duties of the police
- The possible terrorist threats facing the UK

The Judiciary

Judges (who are together called 'the judiciary') are responsible for interpreting the law and ensuring that trials are conducted fairly. The government cannot interfere with this.

Sometimes the actions of the government are claimed to be illegal. If the judges agree, then the government must either change its policies or ask Parliament to change the law. If judges find that a public body is not respecting someone's legal rights, they can order that body to change its practices and/or pay compensation.

Judges also make decisions in disputes between members of the public or organisations. These might be about contracts, property or employment rights or after an accident.

Criminal Courts

There are some differences between the court systems in England and Wales, Scotland and Northern Ireland.

Magistrates' and Justice of the Peace Courts

In England, Wales and Northern Ireland, most minor criminal cases are dealt with in a Magistrates' Court. In Scotland, minor criminal offences go to a Justice of the Peace Court. Magistrates and Justices of the Peace (JPs) are members of the local community. In England, Wales and Scotland they usually work unpaid and do not need legal qualifications. They receive training to do the job and are supported by a legal adviser. Magistrates decide the verdict in each case that comes before them and, if the person is found guilty, the sentence that they are given. In Northern Ireland, cases are heard by a District Judge or Deputy District Judge, who is legally qualified and paid.

Crown Courts and Sheriff Courts

In England, Wales and Northern Ireland, serious offences are tried in front of a judge and a jury in a Crown Court. In Scotland, serious cases are heard in a Sheriff Court with either a sheriff or a sheriff with a jury. The most serious cases in Scotland, such as murder, are heard at a High Court with a judge and jury. A jury is made up of members of the public chosen at random from the local electoral register.

In England, Wales and Northern Ireland a jury has 12 members, and in Scotland a jury has 15 members. Everyone who is summoned to do jury service must do it unless they are not eligible (for example, because they have a criminal conviction) or they provide a good reason to be excused, such as ill health. The jury has to listen to the evidence presented at the trial and then decide a verdict of 'guilty' or 'not guilty' based of what they have heard. In Scotland, a third verdict of 'not proven' is also possible. If the jury finds a defendant guilty, the judge decides the penalty.

Youth Courts

In England, Wales and Northern Ireland, if an accused person is aged 10 to 17, the case is normally heard in a Youth Court in front of up to three specially trained magistrates or a District Judge. The most serious cases will go to the Crown Court. The parents or carers of the young person are expected to attend the hearing. Members of the public are not allowed in Youth Courts, and the name or photographs of the accused young person cannot be published in newspapers or used by the media.

In Scotland a system called the Children's Hearings System is used to deal with children and young people who have committed an offence. Northern Ireland has a system of youth conferencing to consider how a child should be dealt with when they have committed an offence.

Civil Courts

County Courts deal with a wide range of civil disputes. These include people trying to get back money that is owed to them, cases involving personal injury, family matters, breaches of contract, and divorce. In Scotland, most of these matters are dealt with in the Sheriff Court. More serious civil cases – for example, when a large amount of compensation is being claimed – are dealt with in the High Court of England, Wales and Northern Ireland. In Scotland, they are dealt with in the Court of Session in Edinburgh.

The Small Claims Procedure

The small claims procedure is an informal way of helping people to settle minor disputes without spending a lot of time and money using a lawyer. This procedure is used for claims of less than £5,000 in England and Wales and £3,000 in Scotland and Northern Ireland. The hearing is held in front of a judge in an ordinary room, and people from both sides of the dispute sit around a table. Small claims can also be issued online through Money Claims Online (www.moneyclaim.gov.uk). You can get details about the small claims procedure from your local County Court or Sheriff Court.

Legal Advice

Solicitors are trained lawyers who give advice on legal matters, take action for their clients and represent their clients in court. There are solicitors' offices throughout the UK. It is important to find out which aspects of law a solicitor specialises in and to check that they have the right experience to help you with your case. Many advertise in local newspapers and in Yellow Pages. The Citizens Advice Bureau (www.citizensadvice.org.uk) can give you names of local solicitors and which areas of law they specialise in. You can also get this information from the Law Society (www.lawsociety.org.uk) in England and Wales, the Law Society of Scotland (www.lawscot.org.uk) or the Law Society of Northern Ireland (www.lawsoc-ni.org). Solicitors' charges are usually based on how much time they spend of a case. It is very important to find out at the start how much a case is likely to cost.

Check that you understand

- The role of the judiciary
- About the different criminal courts in the UK
- About the different civil courts in the UK
- How you can settle a small claim

Fundamental principles

Britain has a long history of respecting an individual's rights and ensuring essential freedoms. These rights have their roots in Magna Carta, the Habeas Corpus Act and the Bill of Rights of 1689, and they have developed over a period of time. British diplomats and lawyers had an important role in drafting the European Convention on Human Rights and Fundamental Freedoms. The UK was one of the first countries to sign the Convention in 1950.

Some of the principles included in the European Convention of Human Rights are:

- right to life
- prohibition of torture
- prohibition of slavery and forced labour
- right to liberty and security
- right to a fair trial
- freedom of thought, conscience and religion
- freedom of expression (speech).

The Human Rights Act 1998 incorporated the European Convention of Human Rights into UK law. The government, public bodies and the courts must follow the principles of the Convention.

Equal opportunities

UK laws ensure that people are not treated unfairly in any area of life or work because of their age, disability, sex, pregnancy and maternity, race, religion or belief, sexuality or marital status. If you face problems with discrimination, you can get more information from the Citizens Advice Bureau or from one of the following organisations:

• England and Wales: Equality and Human Rights Commission (www.equalityhumanrights.com)

• Scotland: Equality and Human Rights Commission in Scotland (www.equalityhumanrights.com/scotland/the-commission-in-scotland) and Scottish Human Rights Commission (www.scottishhumanrights.com)

• Northern Ireland: equality Commission for Northern Ireland (www.equalityni.org) • Northern Ireland Human Rights Commission (www.nihrc.org).

Domestic violence

In the UK, brutality and violence in the home is a serious crime. Anyone who is violent towards their partner – whether they are a man or a woman, married or living together – can be prosecuted. Anyone who forces another person to have sex, including husbands, wives and civil partners, can be charged with rape.

It is important for anyone facing domestic violence to get help as soon as possible. A solicitor or the Citizens Advice Bureau can explain the available options.

Female Genital Mutilation

Female genital mutilation (FGM), also known as cutting or female circumcision, is illegal in the UK. Practicing FGM or taking a girl or woman abroad for FGM is a criminal offence.

Forced marriage

A marriage should be entered into with the full and free consent of both people involved. Arranged marriages, where both parties agree to the marriage, are acceptable in the UK.

Forced marriage is where one or both parties do not or cannot give their consent to enter into the partnership. Forcing another person to marry is a criminal offence. Forced Marriage Protection Orders were introduced in 2008 for England, Wales and Northern Ireland under the Forced Marriage (Civil Protection) Act 2007.

Court orders can be obtained to protect a person from being forced into a marriage, or to protect a person in a forced marriage. Similar Protection Orders were introduced in Scotland in November

2011. A potential victim, or someone acting for them, can apply for an order. Anyone found to have breached an order can be jailed for up to two years for contempt of court.

Income Tax

Income tax People in the UK have to pay tax on their income, which includes: Wages from paid employment, Profits from self-employment, Taxable benefits, Pensions, Income from property, savings and dividends. Money raised from income tax pays for government services such as roads, education, police and the armed forces. For most people, the right amount of income tax is automatically taken from their income from employment by their employer and paid directly to HM Revenue & Customs (HMRC), the government department that collects taxes. This system is called "Pay As You Earn" (PAYE). If you are self-employed, you need to pay your own tax through a system called 'self-assessment', which includes completing a tax return. Other people may also need to complete a tax return. If HMRC sends you a tax return, it is important to complete and return the form as soon as you have all the necessary information.

National Insurance

Almost everybody in the UK who is in paid work, including self-employed people, must pay National

Insurance Contributions. The money raised from National Insurance Contributions is used to pay for state benefits and services such as the state retirement pension and the National Health Service (NHS).

Employees have their National Insurance Contributions deducted from their pay by their employer. People who are self-employed need to pay National Insurance Contributions themselves. Anyone who does not pay enough National Insurance Contributions will not be able to receive certain contributory benefits such as Jobseeker's Allowance or a full state retirement pension. Some workers, such as part-time workers, may not qualify for statutory payments such as maternity pay if they do not earn enough.

Getting a National Insurance Number

A National Insurance number is a unique personal account number. It makes sure that the National Insurance Contributions and tax you pay are properly recorded against your name. All young people in the UK are sent a National Insurance number just before their 16th birthday. A non-UK national living in the UK and looking for work, starting work or setting up as self-employed will need a National Insurance number.

However, you can start work without one. If you have permission to work in the UK, you will need to telephone the Department for Work and Pensions (DWP) to arrange to get a National Insurance number. You may be required to attend an interview. The DWP will advise you of the appropriate application process and tell you which documents you will need to bring to an interview if one is necessary. You will usually need documents that prove your identity and that you have permission to work in the UK. A National Insurance number does not on its own prove to an employer that you have the right to work in the UK.

Driving

In the UK, you must be at least 17 years to drive a car or motor cycle and you must have a driving licence to drive on public roads. To get a UK driving licence you must pass a driving test, which tests both your knowledge and your practical skills. You need to be at least 16 years old to ride a moped, and there are other age requirements and special tests for driving large vehicles. Drivers can use their driving licence until they are 70 years old. After that, the licence is valid for three years at a time. In Northern Ireland, a newly qualified driver must display an 'R' plate (for restricted driver) for one year after passing the test. If your driving licence if from a country in the European Union (EU), Iceland, Liechtenstein or Norway, you can drive in the UK for as long as your licence is valid.

If you have a licence from any other country, you may use it in the UK for up to 12 months. To continue driving after that, you must get a UK full driving licence. If you are resident in the UK, your car or motor cycle must be registered at the Driver and Vehicle Licensing Agency (DVLA). You must pay an annual road tax and display the tax disc, which shows that the tax has been paid, on the windowscreen.

You must also have valid motor insurance. It is a serious criminal offence to drive without insurance. If your vehicle is over three years old, you must take it to the Ministry of Transport (MOT) test every year. It is an offense not to have a MOT certificate if your vehicle is more than three years old.

Check that you understand

· The fundamental principle of UK law
· That domestic violence, FGM and forced marriage are illegal in the UK
· The system of income tax and National Insurance
· The requirements for driving a car

Your Role in the Community

Becoming a British citizen or settling in the UK brings responsibilities but also opportunities. Everyone has the opportunity to participate in their community. This section looks at some of the responsibilities of being a citizen and gives information about how you can help to make your community a better place to live and work. Values and responsibilities Although Britain is one of the world's most diverse societies, there is a set of shared values and responsibilities that everyone can agree with.

These values and responsibilities include:
· To obey and respect the law
· To be aware of the rights of others and respect those rights
· To treat others with fairness
· To behave responsibly
· To help and protect your family
· To respect and preserve the environment
· To treat everyone equally, regardless of sex, race, religion, age, disability, class or sexual orientation
· To work to provide for yourself and your family
· To help others
· To vote in local and national government elections. Taking on these values and responsibilities will make it easier for you to become a full and active citizen.

Being a Good Neighbor

When you move into a new house or apartment, introduce yourself to the people who live near you. Getting to know your neighbors can help you to become part of the community and make friends. Your neighbors are also a good source of help – for example, they may be willing to feed your pets if you are away, or offer advice on local shops and services. You can help prevent any problems and conflicts with your neighbors by respecting their privacy and limiting how much noise you make. Also try to keep your garden tidy, and only put your refuse bags and bins on the street or in communal areas if they are due to be collected.

Getting Involved in Local Activities

Volunteering and helping your community are an important part of being a good citizen. They enable you to integrate and get to know other people. It helps to make your community a better place if residents support each other. It also helps you to fulfil your duties as a citizen, such as behaving responsibly and helping others.

Helping in Schools

If you have children, there are many ways in which you can help at their schools. Parents can often help in classrooms, by supporting activities or listening to children read. Many schools organise events to raise money for extra equipment or out-of school activities. Activities might include book sales, toy sales or bringing food to sell. You might have good ideas of your own for raising money. Sometimes events are organised by parent-teacher associations (PTAs). Volunteering to help with their events or joining the association is a way of doing something good for the school and also making new friends in your local community. You can find out about these opportunities from notices in the school or notes your children bring home.

School Governors and School Boards

School governors, or members of the school board in Scotland, are people from the local community who wish to make a positive contribution to their children's education. They must be aged 18 or over at the date of their election or appointment. There is no upper age limit. Governors and school boards have an important part to play in raising school standards. They have three key roles:

· Setting the strategic direction of the school
· Ensuring accountability
· Monitoring and evaluating school performance.

You can contact your local school to ask if they need a new governor or school board member. In England, you can also apply online at the School Governors' One-Stop Shop at www.sgoss.org.uk In England, parents and other community groups can apply to open a free school in their local area.

Supporting Political Parties

Political parties welcome new members. Joining one is a way to demonstrate your support for certain views and to get involved in the democratic process. Political parties are particularly busy at election times. Members work hard to persuade people to vote for their candidates – for instance, by handing out leaflets in the street or by knocking on people's doors and asking for their support.

This is called 'canvassing'. You don't have to tell a canvasser how you intend to vote if you don't want to.

Helping with Local Services

There are opportunities to volunteer with a wide range of local service providers, including local hospitals and youth projects. Services often want to involve local people in decisions about the way in which they work. Universities, housing associations, museums and arts councils may advertise for people to serve as volunteers in their governing bodies. You can volunteer with the police, and become a special constable or a lay (non-police) representative. You can also apply to become a magistrate. You will often find advertisements for vacancies in your local newspaper or on local radio.

Blood and Organ Donation

Donated blood is used by hospitals to help people with a wide range of injuries and illnesses.

Giving blood only takes about an hour to do. You can register to give blood at:
· England and North Wales: www.blood.co.uk
· Rest of Wales: www.welsh-blood.org.uk
· Scotland: www.scotblood.co.uk
· Northern Ireland: www.nibts.org

Many people in the UK are waiting for organ transplants. If you register to be an organ donor, it can make it easier for your family to decide whether to donate your organs when you die. You can register to be an organ donor at www.organdonation.nhs.uk. Living people can also donate a kidney.

Other Ways to Volunteer

Volunteering is working for good causes without payment. There are many benefits to volunteering, such as meeting new people and helping make your community a better place. Some volunteer activities will give you a chance to practise your English or develop work skills that will help you find or improve your curriculum vitae (CV). Many people volunteer simply because they want to help other people.

Activities you can do as a volunteer include:

• working with animals – for example, caring for animals at a local rescue shelter
• youth work – for example, volunteering at a youth group
• helping improve the environment – for example, participating in a litter pick-up in the local area • working with the homeless in, for example, a homelessness shelter
• mentoring – for example, supporting someone who has just come out of prison
• work in health and hospitals – for example, working on an information desk in a hospital
• helping older people at, for example, a residential care home.

There are thousands of active charities and voluntary organizations in the UK. They work to improve the lives of people, animals and the environment in many different ways. They range from the British Red Cross, to small local charities working in particular areas. They include charities working with older people (such as Age UK), with children (for example, the National Society for the Prevention of Cruelty to Children (NSPCC)), and with the homeless (for example, Crisis and Shelter). There are also medical research charities (for example, Cancer Research UK), environmental charities (including the National Trust and Friends of the Earth) and charities working with animals (such as the People's Dispensary for Sick Animals (PDSA)).

Volunteers are needed to help with their activities and to raise money. The charities often advertise in local newspapers, and most have websites that include information about their opportunities. You can also get information about volunteering for different organisations from www.do-it.org.uk

There are many opportunities for younger people to volunteer and receive accreditation which will help them to develop their skills. These include the National Citizen Service programme, which gives 16- and 17-year-olds the opportunity to enjoy outdoor activities, develop their skills and take part in a community project.

You can find out more about these opportunities as follows:

- National Citizen Service: at nationalcitizenservice.direct.gov.uk
- England: at www.vinspired.com
- Wales: at www.gwirvol.org
- Scotland: at www.vds.org.uk
- Northern Ireland: at www.volunteernow.co.uk

Looking After the Environment

It is important to recycle as much of your waste as you can. Using recycled materials to make new products uses less energy and means that we do not need to extract more raw materials from the earth. It also means that less rubbish is created, so the amount being put into landfill is reduced. You can learn more about recycling and it benefits at www.recyclenow.com. At this website you can also find out what you can recycle at home and in the local area you live in England. This information is available for Wales at www.wasteawarenesswales.org.uk, for Scotland at www.recycleforscotland.com and for Northern Ireland from your local authority.

A good way to support your local community is to shop for products locally where you can. This will help businesses and farmers in your area in Britain. It will also reduce your carbon footprint, because the products you buy will not have had to travel as far.

Walking and using public transport to get around when you can is also a good way to protect the environment. It means that you create less pollution than when you use a car.

Check that you understand

• The different ways you can help at your child's school
• The role of school governors and members of school boards, and how you can become one • The role of members of political parties

· The different local services people can volunteer to support
· How to donate blood and organs
· The benefit of volunteering for you, other people and the community
· The types of activities that volunteers can do
· How you can look after the environment

Practice Test 1

1 Which of the following is NOT a role of the King:

A To inaugurate important business in the UK
B To receive foreign ambassadors and high commissioners
C To entertain visiting heads of state
D To make state visits overseas

2 Is the statement below TRUE or FALSE?

The Speaker is a neutral MP and does not represent a political party.

3 Who has control over policy and laws governing defence, foreign affairs, immigration, taxation and social security in Northern Ireland?

A The Irish government
B The central UK government
C The Northern Ireland Assembly
D The monarch

4 Is the statement below TRUE or FALSE?

The devolved governments in Scotland, Wales and Northern Ireland cannot control policies and laws governing taxation and social security.

5 Which British sportsman was captain of the English cricket team?

A Bobby Moore
B Sir Ian Botham
C Sir Steve Redgrave
D Sir Jackie Steward

6 In which Japanese cities did the United States drop atomic bombs in August 1945?

A Osaka and Nagasaki
B Hiroshima and Osaka
C Osaka and Kyoto
D France

7 Which of the following countries does not take part in the Six Nations Championship?

A Wales
B Italy
C Germany
D France

8 When was the National Trust founded?

A 1890
B 1895
C 1980
D 1910

9 Where is Loch Lomond and the Trossachs National Park located?

A East of Wales
B West of Wales
C West of Scotland
D East of Scotland

10 By what TWO other names is the Church of England known?

A The Anglican Church
B The Union Church
C The Greatest Church
D The Episcopal Church

11 What day does Lent start?

A On Shrove Tuesday
B On Ash Wednesday
C On Easter Monday
D On Easter Sunday

12 What time do pubs usually open on Sundays in the UK?

A 10 am
B 11 am
C 12 pm
D 1 pm

13 In which period did British Film studios flourish?

A 1920
B 1930
C 1940
D 1950

14 Which of these statements is correct?

A Magistrates must be specially trained legal experts who have been solicitors for three years.
B Magistrates usually work unpaid and do not need legal qualifications

15 The Victorian period famously saw reformers leading moves to improve conditions for which section of society?

A The aristocracy
B The clergy
C The middle classes
D The poor

16 At which festival are mince pies traditionally eaten?

A Christmas
B Diwali
C Easter

D Vaisakhi

17 Which of these statements is correct?

A All the national saints' days are celebrated but only in England and Wales are they official holidays.
B All the patron saints' days are celebrated but only in Scotland and Northern Ireland are they official holidays.

18 Which of the following is a core value of the civil service?

A Bribery
B Integrity
C Laziness
D Party loyalty

19 Is the statement below TRUE or FALSE?

The Commonwealth has no power over its members, although it can suspend membership.

20 Which of the following statements regarding the Black Death is NOT true?

A One third of the population of England died and a similar proportion in Scotland and Wales

B It was one of the worst disasters ever to strike Britain
C It affected children and old people only
D Following the Black Death, there were labour shortages

21 Which of these statements is correct?

A Shakespeare wrote 'To be or not to be'.
B Shakespeare wrote 'We will fight them on the beaches.

22 Which work of music did Benjamin Britten not write?

A A Young Person's Guide to the Orchestra
B Billy Budd
C Peter Grimes
D The Planets

23 Which TWO of the following are environmental charities?

A Crisis
B The National Trust
C Friends of the Earth
D PDSA

24 What countries does 'Great Britain' refer to?

A England and Scotland
B England, Scotland and Northern Ireland

C England, Scotland and Wales
D Just England

Practice Test 2

1 Who was the leader of the Labour Party who introduced a Scottish Parliament and a Welsh Assembly?

A James Callaghan
B Clement Attlee
C Gordon Brown
D Tony Blair

2 What is the maximum amount you can claim through the small claims procedure in Scotland and Northern Ireland?

A £3,000
B £5,000
C £8,000
D £10,000

3 The action of handing out leaflets in the street or knocking on people's doors to ask for their political support is known as:

A Shadowing
B Canvassing
C Marketing
D Persuasion

4 Who should you contact to report a terrorist activity?

A Your local Council.
B Your local MP.
C Your local police force.
D The Prime Minister.

5 During the Middle Ages, England was an important trading nation and people came to England from abroad to trade and also to work. Where did the canal builders come from?

A Germany
B Holland
C France
D Italy

6 Which Paralympic athlete has won gold medals for swimming at the 2008, 2012 and 2016 Paralympic Games?

A Sophie Christiansen
B Ellie Simmonds
C Baroness Tanni Grey-Thompson
D David Weir

7 Which of the following is a charity that works with old people?

A Shelter
B Age UK
C Crisis UK
D Cancer Research UK

8 Isambard Kingdom Brunel was responsible for:

A The construction of the Great Western Railway.
B The invention of the television.
C The construction of the Tower of London.
D The discovery of insulin.

9 Where is the office of the MPs located?

A 10 Downing Street
B The House of Commons
C The House of Lords
D Buckingham Palace

10 What did Isaac Newton discover?

A Gravity
B Penicillin
C Insulin
D Lightbulb

11 What kind of movies did Academy Award winner Nick Park specialise in?

A Action movies
B Animated movies
C Thrillers

D Horror movies

12 Which of the following days are public holidays in Scotland (choose TWO options)?

A 1st of January
B 24th of December
C 3rd of January
D 2nd of January

13 In which of the following matters the Scottish Parliament CANNOT legislate?

A Health
B Education
C Immigration
D Planning

14 Is the statement below TRUE or FALSE?

The House of Commons is normally more independent of the government than the House of Lords

15 Will a non-UK national living in the UK and looking for work, starting work or setting up as self-employed need a National Insurance number?

A Yes
B No

16 When was the Turing machine discovered?

A In the 1920s
B In the 1930s
C In the 1940s
D In the 1950s

17 Which of the following is NOT a
responsibility of the MPs?

A Scrutinise and comment on what the
government is doing
B Represent everyone in the constituency
C Protect life and property
D Debate important national issues

18 During which period were the House of
Lords and House of Commons established?

A Middle Ages
B Iron Age
C The Roman Invasion
D The Anglo-Saxon Invasion

19 Is the statement below TRUE or FALSE?

*The right to a fair trial is not included amongst
the principles of the European Convention of
Human Rights*

20 In the new Church of England created by Henry VIII, who had the power to appoint bishops and order how people should worship?

A The Pope
B The King
C The Prime Minister
D The Archbishop of Canterbury

21 Which of the following is NOT protected by the laws of discrimination?

A Traditional customs
B Disability
C Pregnancy and Maternity
D Religion or Belief

22 Is the statement below TRUE or FALSE?

In Wales, many people speak Gaelic – a completely different language from English – and it is taught in schools and universities:

23 How many years did Queen Victoria reign for?

A Only two years
B Almost 64 years
C Less than two years
D Almost 50 years

24 When did the UK sign the European Convention of Human Rights?

A 1940
B 1945
C 1950
D 1955

Practice Test 3

1 Is the statement below TRUE or FALSE?

Membership to the Commonwealth is compulsory for its members

2 How many verdicts are possible in trials in Scotland?

A Two: 'guilty' or 'not guilty'
B Three: 'guilty', 'not guilty' or 'not proven'
C Three: 'guilty', 'not guilty' or 'on hold'
D Two: 'guilty' or 'not proven'

3 What was the name of the European Union when it was first established?

A European Political Union
B Union of European Countries
C European Economic Community
D Europe United

4 Which of the following charities works with sick animals?

A PDSA
B NSPCC
C Crisis
D Age UK

5 Is the statement below TRUE or FALSE?

Arranged marriages are not acceptable in the UK

6 What is the opposition?

A The second largest party in the House of Lords
B The third largest party in the House of Commons
C The second largest party in the House of Commons
D The third largest party in the House of Lords

7 Which of the following is the responsibility of the Home Secretary?

A Crime, policing and immigration
B Managing relationships with foreign countries
C Education and health
D National and international defence

8 What is the money raised from the Income Tax used for (choose THREE options)?

A Education
B The National Grid system
C Police and the Armed Forces

D Roads

9 Is the statement below TRUE or FALSE?

*Anyone who is violent towards their partner –
whether they are a man or a woman, married
or living together – can be prosecuted.*

10 Is the statement below TRUE or FALSE?

*The Speaker is a neutral MP and does not
represent a political party*

11 Many MPs, Assembly Members, MSPs and
MEPs hold regular local events where
constituents can go in person to talk about
issues that are of concern to them. These are
known as:

A Hansard
B Local 'surgeries'
C Local 'meetings'
D Constituents 'reunions'

12 Where does the Scottish Parliament sit?

A In Glasgow
B In St Andrews
C In Edinburgh
D In Aberdeen

13 During which century did modern tennis

evolve in England?

A 18th century
B 17th century
C 16th century
D 19th century

14 Is the statement below TRUE or FALSE?

The police force is a private service that helps and protects everyone.

15 If you are arrested and taken to a police station, a police officer should

A Make a copy of your ID and retain you until your lawyer arrives
B Tell you the reason for your arrest and that you will be able to seek legal advice
C Offer you a cup of tea
D Explain the law to you and wait for your family to arrive

16 By what other name is the Conservative Party also known as?

A The Labour Party
B The Tudors
C The Green Party
D The Tories

17 Which of the following four changes did the Chartists NOT campaign for?

A For any man to be able to stand as MP
B Secret ballots
C Elections every six years
D For MPs to be paid

18 When did Adolf Hitler come to power in Germany?

A In 1922
B In 1931
C In 1933
D In 1942

19 Which political party does the Speaker represent?

A The Liberal Democrats
B The Conservative party
C The Labour Party
D They do not represent any political party

20 What British actor was best known for his roles in various Shakespeare plays?

A Sir Laurence Olivier
B Joseph Turner
C Andrew Lloyd Webber
D Tim Rice

21 Who defeated the French at the battle of Agincourt in 1415?

A King Edward I of England
B William III of England
C Henry VIII
D King Henry V

22 How many British casualties were recorded during the First World War?

A More than 2 million people
B More than 3 million people
C More than 4 million people
D More than 5 million people

23 What proportion of the population died as a result of the Black Death in England?

A Half of the population
B One third of the population
C 55% of the population
D One quarter of the population

24 What is the meaning of 'Magna Carta'?

A The Big Charter
B The Great Charter
C The King's Charter
D The Small Charter

Practice Test 4

1 How often do the ministers that form the Cabinet meet to make important decisions about government policy?

A Every day
B Weekly
C Monthly
D Every six months

2 When did Emmeline Pankhurst die?

A 1928
B 1935
C 1936
D 1930

3 Which of the following statements is true?

A The police force is a public service that helps and protects everyone
B The police force is a private service that helps and protects everyone
C The police force is a private service in charge of rescuing people from dangerous situations
D The police force is a public service that works to avoid road accidents

4 Is the statement below TRUE or FALSE?

The decade of the 1960s was a period of

significant social change, when there was growth in British fashion, cinema and popular music

5 People in the UK do NOT have to pay tax on

A Income from expensive gifts
B Income from savings
C Income from property
D Pensions

6 When did Henry VIII die?

A In January 1547
B In January 1557
C In February 1547
D In February 1557

7 What Treaty established the European Economic Union in 1957?

A The Treaty of Rome
B The Treaty of Vienna
C The Treaty of Brussels
D The Act of Union

8 When did the late Queen start her reign?

A 1932
B 1349
C 1952
D 1949

9 Which play contains the line "A rose by any other name"

A Romeo and Juliet
B Hamlet
C As You Like It
D Henry V

10 Which British scientist made important discoveries working with steam power?

A David Hume
B Adan Smith
C Alan Turing
D James Watt

11 Which of the following is a British invention from the 20th century?

A The Harrier jump jet
B Radon
C Paraffin wax
D The lightbulb

12 How many members does the Northern Ireland Assembly have?

A 129
B 128
C 118
D 90

13 How much do you have to pay to visit the

Palace of Westminster?

A £20
B £5
C £15
D The entrance to the Palace of Westminster is free

14 How can you visit the Scottish Parliament?

A Arranging a tour through the visitor services
B Contacting the Education Service
C Contacting an AM
D Contacting an MP

15 During the 17th century there were two main groups in Parliament, which were known as:

A The Whigs and the Tories
B The Liberal Democrats and the Labour Party
C The lefties and the right wing
D The Conservative Party and the Liberal Democrats

16 When was the Women's Social and Political Union (WSPU) established?

A 1889
B 1901
C 1899
D 1903

17 Which of the Houses is more important in today's Britain?

A The House of York
B The House of Commons
C The House of Lords
D The House of Lancaster

18 In which city can you find the Scottish Exhibition and Conference Centre (SECC)?

A Edinburgh
B Leeds
C Newcastle
D Glasgow

19 What do new citizens have to swear or affirm as part of the citizenship ceremony?

A They will remain in the UK
B Loyalty to the King
C Loyalty to the Pope
D They will go to church at least once a week

20 What was the biggest source of employment in Britain before the 18th century?

A The ship industry
B Agriculture
C Teaching
D Manufacturing jobs

21 In which TWO cases may a person who has been summoned to do jury service be exempted from doing it

A If they have a criminal conviction
B If they have children
C If they provide a good reason to be excused, such as ill health
D If they have to go to work

22 Which of the following countries did NOT join the European Economic Community when it was first formed in 1957 (choose ONE option)?

A Luxembourg
B West Germany
C The UK
D The Netherlands

23 Who appoints the members of the Cabinet?

A The King
B The Prime Minister
C The Prince of Wales
D The Magistrates

24 During the Crusades, European Christians fought for the control of:

A England
B Ireland
C The holy land
D Central Europe

Practice Test 5

1 What is the name of the building where the Scottish Parliament meet?

A Holyrood
B Senedd
C Westminster
D Stormont

2 On which issues can the Northern Ireland Assembly NOT make decisions?

A Education
B Defence
C Agriculture
D Health

3 What do Ian McEwan, Hilary Mantel and Julian Barnes have in common?

A They are British sports players

B They were awarded with the Man Booker Prize for Fiction
C They won a Nobel Prize in Literature
D They were awarded with the Mercury Music Prize

4 How many devolved administrations are there in the UK?

A 2

B 3
C 4
D 5

5 Who was Henry Purcell?

A   A German-born composer
B   An organist at Westminster Abbey
C   An opera composer
D   A jazz musician

6 Which of the following drugs is illegal in the UK?

A Cannabis
B Cocaine
C Ecstasy
D All of the above are illegal

7 Which of the following statements regarding Scottish television is true?

A There is a channel with programmes in the Gaelic language
B There are three channels in the Gaelic language
C All programmes are broadcasted in English
D There are no specific programmes to Scotland

8 What were the working conditions like during the Industrial Revolution?

A Average
B Acceptable
C Best in the World
D Very Poor

9 Who composed a suite of pieces themed around the planets and the solar system called 'The Planets'?

A The Edward Elgar
B George Frederick Handel
C Gustav Holst
D Sir William Walton

10 Which of the following statements is true?

A Proceedings in Parliament are broadcast on television and published in official reports
B Proceedings in Parliament are not broadcast on television but published in official reports
C Proceedings in Parliament are broadcast on the radio and not published in official reports
D Proceedings in Parliament are broadcast on the radio only

11 Which of the following is a musical venue located in London?

A The O2
B Glastonbury
C The Dome
D The Fringe

12 Who directed the movie 'The Killing Fields' in 1984?

A Roland Joffé
B Carol Reed
C David Lean
D Alfred Hitchcock

13 Where can you find copies of the 'Hansard'?

A In the Guardian newspaper
B In large libraries and at www.parliament.uk
C In the bookshop
D In any library

14 Which TWO of the following castles are located in Scotland?

A Conwy Castle
B Caernarfon Castle
C Crathes Castle
D Inveraray Castle

15 How many senior MPs are appointed by the Prime Minister?

A Almost 30
B 15
C Almost 20
D 25

16 What was Charles Chaplin famous for?

A Special effects movies
B Horror movies
C Silent movies
D Murder-mystery movies

17 What was the population of the UK in 2010?

A Just over 50 million
B Just over 62 million
C Just under 50 million
D Just under 60 million

18 Is the statement below TRUE or FALSE?

In the UK, there is a National Lottery for which draws are made every month

19 Is the statement below TRUE or FALSE?

The Muslim festival known as Eid ul Adha reminds Muslims of their own commitment to God

20 When is the Jewish celebration known as Hanukkah normally celebrated?

A June or July
B October or November
C November or December
D March or April

21 When is the Sikh festival which celebrates the founding of the Sikh community (Khalsa) and known as Vaisakhi celebrated?

A 14th of February
B 14th of April
C 30th of March
D 30th of April

22 Who directed the movie 'Brief Encounter' in 1945?

A Alfred Hitchcock
B Hugh Hudson
C Carol Reed
D David Lean

23 Which TWO of the following water sports are popular in the UK?

A Waterpolo
B Rowing
C Sailing
D Surfing

24 According to the 2011 Census, what percentage of the population identified themselves as Hindu?

A 0.5%
B 1%
C 1.5%
D 3%

Practice Test 6

1 Which landscape architect designed grounds around country houses so that the landscape appeared to be natural, with grass, trees and lakes?

A Clarice Cliff
B Lancelot 'Capability' Brown
C Alexander McQueen
D Vivienne Westwood

2 According to the Citizenship Survey carried out in the UK in 2009, what percentage of the population identified themselves as Muslim?

A 1%
B 2%
C 3%
D 4%

3 What is the money from TV licences used for?

A To pay actors and actresses
B To pay for the British Broadcasting Corporation (BBC)
C To pay for publicity
D To pay for private channels

4 Which of the following countries does not

take part in the Six Nations Championship?

A Wales
B Italy
C Germany
D France

5 Which famous poem tells the story of the knights at the court of King Arthur?

A Beowulf
B Paradise Lost
C Sir Gawain and the Green Knight
D King Arthur and his knights

6 Is the statement below TRUE or FALSE?

Eid ul Adha is the day when Muslims thank Allah for giving them the strength to complete the fast

7 Which of the following poets wrote poems inspired by Scotland and the traditional stories and songs from the area on the borders of Scotland and England?

A Geoffrey Chaucer
B William Blake
C Sir Walter Scott
D William Wordsworth

8 Which of the following is a responsibility or freedom shared by all those living in the UK and which people wishing to be a permanent resident or citizen of the UK should respect?

A Go to church
B Treat others with fairness
C Eat traditional British food
D Look after your neighbours

9 Which British writer wrote satirical novels including 'Brideshead Revisited'?

A Evelyn Waugh
B Sir Arthur Conan Doyle
C Sir Kingsley Amis
D Thomas Hardy

10 The longest distance on the mainland in the UK is from John O'Groats on the north coast of Scotland to a location in the south-west corner of England known as:

A Land's Point
B Earth Point
C Eastbourne
D Land's End

11 What is the note with the highest value in the UK?

A £20
B £50
C £100
D £500

12 Which of the following statements is true?

A For some Scottish people, Hogmanay is a bigger holiday than Christmas
B For some Scottish people, Hogmanay is a bigger holiday than New Year's Eve.
C For some Welsh people, Hogmanay is a bigger holiday than Christmas
D For some Irish people, Hogmanay is a bigger holiday than New Year's Eve

13 What is the name of the highest mountain in Wales?

A Lake District
B Snowdon
C South Downs
D Giant's Causeway

14 Who was the captain of the English football team that won the World Cup in 1966?

A David Beckham
B Bobby Moore
C Sir Ian Botham

D Sir Roger Bannister

15 How many volunteers did the National Trust have when it was first formed in 1895?

A 2
B 3
C 200
D 300

16 During the 19th century, the UK was the world's major producer of which THREE materials?

A Coal
B Iron
C Silk
D Cotton cloth

17 Is the statement below TRUE or FALSE?

Bonfire Night remembers the day when a group of Catholics led by Guy Fawkes killed the Protestant king with a bomb in the Houses of Parliament

18 Which of the following movies played an important role in boosting morale during the Second World War?

A The Ladykillers
B Carry on

C Passport to Pimlico
D In Which We Serve

19 Is the statement below TRUE or FALSE?

To be able to vote in England, you have to register at your local council electoral registration office.

20 Where did slaves mainly come from during the slave trade?

A South America
B West Africa
C Southeast Asia
D North Africa

21 What are the key roles of the governors and school boards (select THREE answers)?

A Providing funding for all students
B Setting the strategic direction of the school
C Ensuring accountability
D Monitoring and evaluating school performance

22 Why is it important to recycle (select two answers)?

A Using recycled materials to make new products uses less energy than using raw materials

B It is a criminal offence and you could be arrested if you do not do it
C To reduce the expenses of the local council
D Less rubbish is created, so the amount being put into landfill is reduced

23 What is the most well-known rugby league (club) competition?

A The Grand National
B The All England championship
C The Six Nations championship
D The Super League

24 Which of the following is a traditional character of the pantomimes?

A The gentleman
B The Dame
C A unicorn
D A mermaid

Practice Test 7

1 Nelson's Column in Trafalgar Square, London, is a monument to

A Henry VIII
B Napoleon
C Admiral Nelson
D James I

2 What did Sir Edmond Halley successfully predict?.

A The return of a Comet
B The First World War
C The Second World War
D Admiral Nelson's death.

3 Who was Richard Austen Butler?

A A British economist
B A Welsh poet
C A Labour MP
D A Conservative MP

4 During the Victorian period, the British Empire grew to cover:
Select three answers

A Australia

B Brazil
C India
D Large parts of Africa

5 How can MP's be contacted?

A By Letter
B By Telephone
C Through local 'surgeries'
D All of the above.

6 Where was Isaac Newton from?

A Lincolnshire
B Stratford-upon-Avon
C Cardiff
D Edinburgh

7 Which one of the following is not a British coin?

A 1p
B 2p
C 75p
D £1

8 When did the UK join the EU?

A 1945
B 1973
C 1990
D 1995

9 Which TWO British poets wrote about their experiences in the WWI?

A Lord Byron and Percy Shelley
B John Keats and Alfred Lord Tennyson
C Robert and Elizabeth Browning
D Wilfred Owen and Siegfried Sassoon

10 Which new industries developed in the UK during the Great Depression (choose 2 answers)?

A The metallurgic industry
B The automobile industry
C The shipbuilding industry
D The aviation industry

11 Which Christian festival celebrates the birth of Jesus Christ?

A Easter Sunday
B Remembrance Day
C Boxing Day
D Christmas Day

12 What is the Bessemer process?

A An industrial process for the mass-production of iron
B An industrial process for the mass-production of copper

C An industrial process for the mass-production of titanium
D An industrial process for the mass-production of steel

13 Is the statement below TRUE or FALSE?

More women than men study at university.

14 Which of the following cities is not in Wales?

A Cardiff
B Swansea
C Bradford
D Newport

15 Which of the following sports began in the UK?

A Cricket
B Football
C Rugby
D All of the above

16 Do you need a TV licence for watching TV on a mobile phone?

A Yes
B No

17 Is the statement below TRUE or FALSE?

On average, girls leave school with better qualifications than boys.

18 The development of the Bessemer process during the Industrial Revolution led to the development of which two industries

A Shipbuilding industry
B Chemical industry
C Railways industry
D Car industry

19 Sake Dean Mahomet was born in

A 1756
B 1750
C 1759
D 1760

20 Which Solicitor should a person prefer for his or her case?

A The one with the right experience and expertise that suits the case
B The one with the most age
C The one with the most solved cases
D The one with the most winning cases

21 Which of the following statements is TRUE?

A The official name of the country is the United Kingdom of Great Britain and Southern Ireland.
B The official name of the country is Great Britain and Southern Ireland.
C The official name of the country is the United Kingdom of Great Britain and Northern Ireland.
D The official name of the country is the United Kingdom and Great Ireland.

22 The Romans were responsible for creating

A A structure of law

B Stone carvings
C Westminster Abbey
D The Victorian Empire

23 Who are Mary Quant, Alexander McQueen and Vivienne Westwood?

A Leading fashion designers of recent years in the UK
B Leading models of recent years in the UK
C Leading stylists of recent years in the UK
D Leading makeup artist of recent years in the UK

24 Which of the following aspects, played an important role in the UK?

A Landscaping
B Garden design
C Both A and B
D None of the above

Practice Test 8

1 Who is Sir Terence Conran?

A Apparel Designer
B Interior Designer
C Furniture Designer
D All of the above

2 Which of the following is a designer of furniture from Britain in the 18th century?

A Thomas Chippendale
B Thomas Benjamin
C Thomas Rivers
D Alexander McQueen

3 What does the CBI represent?

A Views of British business
B The Human Rights
C The Environment
D None of the above

4 What does Britain have in its society that everyone can agree with?

A A set of laws that only dominate White people
B A set of shared values and responsibilities
C A typical standardized system
D None of the above

5 Where does every British citizen have the opportunity to participate?

A In their Community
B In their Local Police Station
C In their Local Investigating Operation
D None of the above

6 What do most terrorist groups try to do?

A To radicalise and recruit people to their cause
B To threaten other legal organisations
C To assassinate the higher authorities
D To invade and capture areas of their interest

7 What poses the most serious terrorist threat to the UK?

A Al-Qa'ida and its affiliates
B The Russians
C The Puritans
D The Muslims

8 In Northern Ireland, a system for maintaining electoral register is known as "Individual registration." What happens in it?

A An electoral registration form is sent to every household to be filled
B Every person entitled to vote must complete their own registration form
C Every person entitled to vote will

automatically registered with their details by the government

D None of the above

9 What information do you require to find out which local authority do you belong to?

A Your postcode
B Your national insurance number
C Your phone number
D Your social security number

10 How often is the electoral register updated?

A Every year in a month of January
B Every two years in a month of December
C Every year in a month of September or October
D Every three years in a month of October

11 What is the official law about radio and television coverage of the political parties?

A Air time between the main party and the rivals should be equal
B The main party should get more air time
C There should be no coverage of the rival party
D None of the above

12 Has Britain always been a democracy as we know it?

A Yes, it has been a democracy since the beginning
B No, At the turn of the 19th century, Britain was not a democracy as we know it today
C No, At the turn of the 16th century, Britain was not a democracy as we know it today.
D None of the above

13 In the beginning, what was the status of the reforms that the chartists campaigned for?

A It was successful right from the beginning
B It was generally seen as a failure
C It was rejected right away
D None of the above

14 What is meant by the "Franchise"?

A It is the number of people who have the right to vote
B It is number of people who are representing their districts
C It is a number of electoral districts in the Britain
D It is number of total population of the Britain

15 What was the third reform that the Chartists wanted in the 1830s and 1840s?

A Wales should have more representation in the electoral system
B Ireland must not get more attention than the others
C The Queen's or King's hometown should be given priority over others
D All regions to be equal in the electoral system

16 By 1928, the voting franchise was extended to men and women over what age?

A 15
B 20
C 21
D 25

17 In Northern Ireland some people speak

A Welsh
B Irish Gaelic
C German
D Latin American

18 When was the film "Lawrence of Arabia," directed by David Lean, released?

A In 1960
B In 1962
C In 1963

D In 1964

19 What percentage of people in the UK are Hindu?

A 1%
B 2%
C 3%
D 4%

20 What is the major religion in the UK?

A Muslim
B Indian
C Christian
D No religion

21 Who is allowed to practice their religion in the UK?

A Only Christians
B Only Muslims
C Both A and B
D Everyone is allowed to follow their religion

22 What sort of religious buildings are present in the UK?

A Only churches
B Islamic Mosques
C Hindu Temples
D All of the above

23 Most towns and cities in the United Kingdom have a central shopping area, What do these areas called?

A Town centre
B Central mall
C Marketing area
D Commercial area

24 Who was the inventor of the World Wide Web?

A Sir Tim Berners-Lee
B Sir Peter Mansfield
C Sir Ian Wilmut
D Sir Bernard Lovell

Practice Test 9

1 What does Philosophiae Naturalis Principia Mathematica mean?

A The philosophy of the world
B The philosophy of maths applied to the world
C The philosophy of maths applied to the world
D Mathematical Principle of Natural Philosophy

2 Sir Isaac Newton was a prominent and earliest member of which scientific society?

A Anglican society
B Royal society
C Social society
D Natural society

3 Who discovered that white light is made up of rainbow colours?

A Albert Einstein
B Sir Isaac Newton
C Charles Darwin
D Aristotle

4 What should the police officers must not do?

A Misuse their authority
B Make a false statement
C Be rude or commit racial discrimination
D All of the above

5 Who is appointed by the Police and Crime Commissioner?

A Commander In-Chief
B Local Chief Constable
C Governor General
D Lord Protector

6 How dependent are the police forces of the United Kingdom on the government?

A They are totally dependent on the government
B They are partially dependent on the government
C They are independent of the government
D None of the above

7 What should you do in case you are arrested and taken to the police station?

A Seek legal advice
B Fight with the police officer
C Demand to be released there and then
D All of the above

8 What other option does a voter have if it is

difficult for him or her to get to a polling station or polling place?

A He or she can register for a postal ballot
B He or she can vote on a call
C He or she can send someone else on their behalf
D None of the above

9 Apart from the name and address, what will a voter be asked to show at the polling station in Northern Ireland?

A His or her social security number
B His or her marital status
C His or her age
D His or her photographic identification

10 Which country did not want to join the EEC but eventually did so?

A Canada
B Austria
C The UK
D All of them

11 What is the law in the United Kingdom regarding driving without valid motor insurance?

A It is a criminal offence
B It is acceptable

C It is applauded
D All of them

12 What does the EEC stand for?

A England's Elite Conference
B Europe Empowerment Corporation
C European Economic Community
D None of the above

13 Who played an important role in drafting the European Convention on Human Rights and Fundamental Freedoms in the United Kingdom?

A British Lawyers and Diplomats
B British Citizens
C British Doctors and Dentists
D British Journalists

14 What are the two types of laws in the UK?

A Criminal law and Civil law
B Civil law and legal law
C Both A and B
D Parliamentary law and General law

15 What does the Criminal law relate to?

A Crimes that are usually investigated by the police or another authority
B Crimes that result in casualties

C Disputes between individuals or groups
D All of the above

16 What is the law in the United Kingdom
regarding the buying and selling of drugs like
heroin, cocaine, ecstasy, and cannabis?

A It is legal, if only done by a police officer
B It is legal, if only done by a doctor
C It is legal, under all circumstances
D It is illegal, under all circumstances

17 When was the first television broadcast
between London and Glasgow made?

A 1930
B 1931
C 1932
D 1933

18 What does IVF stand for?

A Institute of Virtual Fashion
B In-Vitro Fertilisation
C Inside Vulnerable Facility
D None of the above

19 What were the pound's economic
conditions in the United Kingdom in the
1970s?

A The pound became the strongest currency
in the world

B The exchange rate between the pound and other currencies became unstable.
C The exchange rate between the pound and other currencies became stable.
D None of the above

20 What influenced industries and services in the United Kingdom during the 1970s, causing conflict between trade unions and the government?

A Unstable exchange rate of the pound
B Strikes
C Civil War
D Inter-city conflicts

21 How did the pound's instability in the 1970s affect the "balance of payments"?

A Imported goods became cheaper than exported
B Imported goods became more costly than the exported
C Imported goods became more common than the exported
D None of the above

22 The 1970s was a time of serious unrest in?

A Northern Ireland
B Netherland
C Scotland

D Wales

23 When the Northern Ireland's parliament
was suspended in 1972, who governed the
country then?

A Common Wealth
B Russian Federation
C Scotland's parliament
D UK government

24 After the Second World War, what huge
task did the British face?

A Reclaiming land
B Rebuilding Britain
C Refugees
D All of the above

Practice Test 10

1 What was encouraged to relieve the labour shortage in the UK during 1950s?

A Overseas Colonization
B Immigration
C War
D All of the above

2 Following WWII, there was a shortage of labor in Britain, and this problem still continued in

A The 1950s
B The 1960s
C The 1970s
D The 1980s

3 Which poem did Dylan Thomas write for his dying father in 1952?

A Under Milk Wood
B Do Not Go Gentle into That Good Night
C A very happy ending
D Romeo and Juliet

4 Which of the following states regarded as Central Power during the First World War?

A Austro-Hungarian Empire
B Ottoman Empire
C Germany

D All of the above

5 Why did the rapid progress in Britain in the early 20th century come to a halt?

A Because the famine hit the Empire
B Because of the plague that nearly half the overall population of Britain
C Because of the Vietnam war
D Because the war broke out between several European nations
6 Which film was directed by Nicolas Roeg in 1973?

A Women in Love
B Don't Look Now
C The Third Man
D Brief Encounter

7 When was the film "Touching the Void," directed by Kevin MacDonald, released?

A In 2000
B In 2003
C In 2006
D In 2009

8 Who was the director of the film "Four Weddings and a Funeral"?

A Ken Russel

B Roland Joffé
C Hugh Hudson
D Mike Newell

9 By the end of which year did the international forces have full security responsibility in all the provinces of Afghanistan?

A 2012
B 2013
C 2014
D 2015

10 When did the "Iraqi Invasion of Kuwait" happen?

A 1989
B 1990
C 1993
D 1995

11 When did the British combat troops leave Iraq?

A 2002
B 2005
C 2009
D 2012

12 What is the purpose of the International Security Assistance Force (ISAF) concerning Afghanistan?

A To ensure that Afghan territory can never again be used as a safe haven for international terrorism
B To ensure that Afghans would never be able to stand up for their own rights
C To develop legislative assemblies in Afghanistan and rule the country
D None of the above

13 When did the UK sign the European Convention of Human Rights?

A 1950
B 1949
C 1948
D 1947

14 When were the British armed forces have been engaged in the global fight against international terrorism?

A 1990
B 2000
C 2010
D 2020

15 What deals with the disputes over wages and cases include unfair dismissal or

discrimination in the workplace?

A Employment Law
B Consumers' Rights Law
C Housing Law
D Criminal Law

16 Where can you find out about the types of crimes in the UK?

A In the local library
B Online at www.gov.uk
C In the Local Police Stations
D All of the above

17 How do a person know where not to smoke in the UK?

A Passersby will let know
B Police officers will tell
C There are signs of no smoking where it is prohibited to smoke
D There are big green signs where it is prohibited to smoke

18 Where do the Housing laws apply?

A To settle disputes about faulty goods or services
B To settle disputes over wages and cases of unfair dismissal or discrimination in the workplace
C To settle disputes between individuals or

groups
D To settle disputes landlords and tenants over issues such as repairs and eviction

19 Which teams does the UK compete against in the UEFA Champions League?

A Teams from Antarctica
B Teams from Africa
C Teams from Asia
D Teams from Europe

20 How many parts of the government are there in the UK?

A A few
B Several
C There are no parts and the government is only one
D The Monarch

21 Which government is present in Scotland, Wales, and Northern Ireland?

A Fully independent governments
B Devolved governments
C Local governments
D All of the above

22 Where are Solicitor's offices in the UK?

A Only in capital cities
B Only in England
C Throughout the UK

D Only with the National courts

23 From where can one get the names of the local solicitors and the areas of law in which they specialise?

A From the local newspaper
B From the Citizens Advice Bureau
C From the Portal of Citizen Relationships
D All of the above

24 What do Solicitors do?

A They give advice on legal matters and represent their clients in court
B They only give advice on legal matters
C They report the cases in courts
D They teach Law in universities

Answers to Practice Test 1

	ANSWER	EXPLANATION
1	A	The King performs various diplomatic duties, including receiving foreign ambassadors and high commissioners, entertaining visiting heads of state, and making state visits abroad in order to strengthen relationships with other countries.
2	TRUE	Although the Speaker is an MP who represents a constituency and addresses the concerns of their constituents like any other MP, they are neutral and do not align with any political party.
3	B	While policy and laws concerning defense, foreign affairs, immigration, taxation, and social security are maintained by the central UK government, other public services such as education are managed by the devolved administrations.
4	TRUE	The central UK government retains control over policy and laws related to defense, foreign affairs, immigration, taxation, and social security. On the other

hand, devolved administrations are responsible for the administration of certain public services, such as education.

5	B	Sir Ian Botham, also known as Beefy, is a retired English cricketer who is widely considered one of the greatest all-rounders in the history of the sport. He played for England in both Test and One Day International matches, and captained the team on several occasions. Botham is known for his aggressive and flamboyant style of play, and holds numerous English Test cricket records, including the most wickets taken by a fast bowler and the most runs scored by a number eight batsman. He is also the only player to score over 5,000 runs and take over 300 wickets in Test matches for England.
6	A	The war between the United States and Japan, which was part of the wider conflict of World War II, ended in August 1945 with the dropping of atomic bombs on the Japanese cities of Hiroshima and Nagasaki. This event marked the first and only time that nuclear weapons have been used in warfare, and it significantly contributed to Japan's surrender and the end of

the war. The bombings caused widespread destruction and loss of life, with estimates of the number of casualties ranging from 129,000 to 226,000. The decision to use atomic weapons remains a controversial topic to this day, with some arguing that it was necessary to end the war and others arguing that it was a grave violation of human rights and international law.

7   C   The Six Nations Championship is an annual international rugby union competition contested by the national teams of England, Ireland, Scotland, Wales, France, and Italy. It is one of the most prestigious and high-profile tournaments in the rugby world, and attracts large crowds and extensive media coverage. The competition has a long history dating back to the late 19th century, and has evolved over the years to become the format it is today. Each team plays the other five teams in a round-robin format, with the team that accumulates the most points being crowned the champion. In addition to the main championship, there are also several other awards and trophies that are contested, including the Triple Crown for the team that defeats the other

three home nations, and the Wooden Spoon for the team that finishes last.

8	B	The National Trust is a conservation organization in that was founded in 1895 by three volunteers: Octavia Hill, Sir Robert Hunter, and Hardwicke Rawnsley. The organization was established in response to concerns about the rapid industrialization and urbanization of the country, and the associated loss of natural and cultural heritage. The National Trust's mission is to protect and promote the conservation of historic places and spaces, as well as the countryside and coast, for the benefit of the public. It accomplishes this through a variety of means, including the acquisition and management of historic buildings, gardens, and landscapes, as well as through education and outreach programs. Today, the National Trust is a major player in the field of conservation in the UK, and is supported by over five million members and thousands of volunteers.
9	C	The Loch Lomond and the Trossachs National Park is a protected area located in the west of Scotland. It covers an

area of approximately 720 square miles (1,865 square kilometers) and includes a range of landscapes, from rolling hills and forests to lochs (lakes) and mountains. The park is home to a wide variety of wildlife, including red deer, golden eagles, and ospreys, and is a popular destination for outdoor activities such as hiking, cycling, and water sports. The park was established in 2002 and is managed by a partnership of organizations, including the Scottish government, local authorities, and conservation groups. Its aim is to protect and promote the natural and cultural heritage of the region, while also providing opportunities for people to enjoy the outdoors.

10   A & D   The Church of England is also known as the Episcopal Church or Anglican Church in other countries. The Church of England is part of the worldwide Anglican Communion, which comprises over 85 million members in 44 member churches around the globe. It is a Protestant Christian denomination that traces its roots back to the 16th century and the English Reformation. The Church of England is known for its liturgical traditions and its

commitment to social justice, and it is the largest Christian denomination in England, with over 26 million members.

| 11 | B | Lent is a period of fasting, repentance, and spiritual discipline observed by Christians, particularly those in the Western tradition. It begins on Ash Wednesday, which is the first day of the season of Lent. Ash Wednesday takes its name from the practice of marking the foreheads of worshippers with ashes as a sign of repentance and mortality. It falls 46 days before Easter (not including Sundays) and is a time for Christians to reflect on their relationship with God and to prepare for the celebration of Easter. During Lent, many Christians observe various forms of asceticism, such as fasting, prayer, and almsgiving, as a way of strengthening their spiritual lives and deepening their relationship with God. |
| 12 | C | Pubs, which are a type of establishment that serves alcoholic beverages and often serves food, are generally open during the day from 11:00 am (12:00 noon on Sundays). Many pubs also offer evening and late-night service, but the specific hours of operation can |

vary. Pubs are a popular social gathering place in many parts of the world, and are often a central part of the local community. They can range in size and style, from small, traditional pubs with a cozy atmosphere to large, modern establishments with a range of amenities. Pubs are known for their relaxed atmosphere, and are often a place for people to socialize, watch sports events, listen to live music, or play games.

| 13 | B | During the 1930s, the British film industry experienced a period of prosperity and growth. British film studios were producing a wide range of films that were popular with audiences both in the UK and abroad. The 1930s saw the emergence of several notable British actors and directors, including Alfred Hitchcock, Charles Laughton, and Vivien Leigh, who went on to become international stars. The decade also saw the release of several classic British films, such as "Gone with the Wind," "Rebecca," and "The 39 Steps," which have had a lasting impact on the film industry and continue to be widely admired today. Overall, the 1930s were an important and influential period for the British film industry, and |

		laid the foundation for its continued success in the decades that followed.
14	B	Magistrates and Justices of the Peace (JPs) are members of the local community. In England, Wales and Scotland they usually work unpaid and do not need legal qualifications.
15	C	Within the UK, the middle classes became increasingly significant and a number of reformers led moves to improve conditions of life for the masses.
16	A	Christmas is celebrated in a traditional way. People usually spend the day at home and eat a special meal, which often includes roast turkey, Christmas pudding and mince pies.
17	B	All the patron saints' days are celebrated but only in Scotland and Northern Ireland are they official holidays.
18	B	Civil servants are expected to carry out their role with dedication and a commitment to the civil service and its core values. These are: integrity, honesty, objectivity and impartiality (including being politically neutral).
19	TRUE	The Commonwealth has no power over its members, although it can suspend membership.

20	C	In 1348, a disease, probably a form of plague, came to Britain. This was known as the Black Death. One third of the population of England died and a similar proportion in Scotland and Wales. This was one of the worst disasters ever to strike Britain. Following the Black Death, the smaller population meant there was less need to grow cereal crops. There were labour shortages and peasants began to demand higher wages.
21	A	Lines from his plays and poems which are often still quoted include: -Once more unto the breach (Henry V) ; -To be or not to be (Hamlet) ; -A rose by any other name(Romeo and Juliet) ; -All the world's a stage (As you like it) ; -The darling buds of May (Sonnet 18- Shall I Compare Thee To A Summer's Day).
22	D	Edward Benjamin Britten, Baron Britten OM CH (22 November 1913 – 4 December 1976, aged 63) was an English composer, conductor, and pianist. He was a central figure of 20th-century British music, with a range of works including opera, other vocal music, orchestral and chamber pieces. His best-known

works include the opera Peter Grimes, Billy Bud and the orchestral showpiece The Young Person's Guide to the Orchestra.

| 23 | B & C | The National Trust and Friends of the Earth are environmental charities. |
| 24 | C | Great Britain' refers only to England, Scotland and Wales, not to Northern Ireland. |

Answers to Practice Test 2

	ANSWER	EXPLANATION
1	D	In 1997 the Labour Party led by Tony Blair was elected. The Blair government introduced a Scottish Parliament and a Welsh Assembly.
2	A	The small claims procedure is an informal way of helping people to settle minor disputes without spending a lot of time and money using a lawyer. This procedure is used for claims of less than £10,000 in England and Wales and £3,000 in Scotland and Northern Ireland.
3	B	The action of handing out leaflets in the street or knocking on people's doors to ask for their political support is known as canvassing.
4	C	If you think someone is trying to persuade you to join an extremist or terrorist cause, you should notify your local police force.
5	B	During the Middle Ages, England was an important trading nation and people came to England from abroad to trade and also to work. Canal builders came from Holland.
6	B	Ellie Simmonds is a Paralympian who won gold medals for

		swimming at the 2008, 2012 and 2016 Paralympic Games and holds a number of world records. She was the youngest member of the British team at the 2008 Games.
7	B	Age UK is a charity that works with old people.
8	A	Brunel was originally from Portsmouth, England. He was an engineer who built tunnels, bridges, railway lines and ships. He was responsible for constructing the Great Western Railway, which was the first major railway built in Britain. It runs from Paddington Station in London to the south west of England, the West Midlands and Wales.
9	B	The MP's office is located at The House of Commons, Westminster, London, SW1A OAA.
10	A	Newton's most famous published work was Philosophiae Naturalis Principia Mathematica ('Mathematical Principle of Natural Philosophy'), which showed how gravity applied to the whole universe. Newton also discovered that white light is made up of the colours of the rainbow.
11	B	Britain continues to be particularly strong in special effects and animation. One

example is the work of Nick Park, who has won four Oscars for his animated films, including three for films featuring Wallace and Gromit.

12	A & D	In Scotland, January 1st and 2nd are officially recognized as public holidays. This means that banks and other financial institutions are closed, and many businesses may also be closed. These holidays are generally used as an opportunity for people to relax and celebrate the start of the new year.
13	C	The Scottish Parliament has the authority to make laws on a range of issues, including civil and criminal law, healthcare, education, land use planning, and taxation. The Parliament has the power to legislate on these matters in order to promote the well-being of the people of Scotland and to ensure that the country is governed effectively.
14	FALSE	The House of Lords, which is one of the two chambers of the Parliament of the United Kingdom, is typically more independent from the government than the House of Commons, which is the other chamber. This means that members of the House of Lords are not directly elected by the public and are not beholden to

the same political parties as members of the House of Commons. As a result, they may be more likely to take a broader perspective on issues and to act as a check on the government's power.

15   A   If you are a non-UK national living in the United Kingdom and seeking employment, starting a job, or establishing yourself as self-employed, you will need to obtain a National Insurance number. This number is a unique identifier that is used for tax and social security purposes. It is important to note, however, that you can begin working without a National Insurance number, although you may need to provide evidence that you are eligible to work in the UK. You can apply for a National Insurance number through the Department for Work and Pensions.

16   B   Alan Turing, a British mathematician who lived from 1912 to 1954, invented the concept of a Turing machine in the 1930s. A Turing machine is a theoretical device used in mathematical logic and computer science to study the concept of computation. It is a simple, abstract machine that can be used to model the logic of any

computer algorithm. Despite its simplicity, the Turing machine has had a profound impact on the field of computer science and is considered a cornerstone of theoretical computer science.

17   C   Members of Parliament (MPs) have a variety of duties and roles. They are elected to represent the people living in their constituencies, which means that they are responsible for advocating for their constituents' needs and concerns. MPs also have a role in the legislative process, as they work to create new laws and modify existing ones. Additionally, MPs are expected to closely monitor and scrutinize the actions of the government, and to provide commentary and criticism when appropriate. Finally, MPs are expected to engage in debates on important national issues and to contribute to the overall functioning of the government.

18   A   During the Middle Ages, the size of the English Parliament grew and it became necessary to divide it into two distinct chambers: the House of Commons and the House of Lords. The House of Commons was composed of elected representatives of the common people, while the House of Lords

was made up of high-ranking nobles, bishops, and other members of the aristocracy. Both houses played important roles in the legislative process and in shaping the policies of the government. The development of these two houses marked the beginning of the modern parliamentary system in England.

| 19 | FALSE | The right to a fair trial is a fundamental principle of the European Convention on Human Rights, which is a treaty that protects the human rights of individuals in countries that are party to the Convention. The right to a fair trial is considered to be one of the most important protections for individuals accused of crimes, as it ensures that they are treated fairly and are given the opportunity to defend themselves against the allegations against them. The principle of a fair trial is essential for ensuring that justice is served and that the rights of the accused are protected. |
| 20 | B | In the Church of England, which was established during the English Reformation, the monarch (the king or queen) was given the authority to appoint bishops and to determine the way in which people were to worship. This marked a |

significant shift in power, as previously the Pope had held these powers in the Roman Catholic Church. The new Church of England was established as a result of King Henry VIII's desire to obtain a divorce from his wife, Catherine of Aragon, which the Pope refused to grant. The creation of the Church of England allowed Henry to break away from the Roman Catholic Church and establish a national church that was independent from Rome.

| 21 | A | In the United Kingdom, laws are in place to protect individuals from discrimination on the basis of their age, disability, gender, pregnancy and maternity status, race, religion or belief, sexual orientation, and marital status. These laws ensure that people are treated fairly and with respect in all aspects of life, including in the workplace. The goal of these laws is to promote equality and to prevent individuals from being unfairly disadvantaged due to their personal characteristics or circumstances. |
| 22 | FALSE | In Wales, a significant portion of the population speaks Welsh, which is a distinct language with its own unique grammar and vocabulary. Welsh is spoken by a majority of people in some areas |

of Wales and is also taught in schools and universities throughout the country. Many people in Wales take pride in their Welsh heritage and language, and there are various initiatives in place to promote and support the use of Welsh.

23	B	Queen Victoria ascended to the throne of the United Kingdom in 1837 at the age of 18, following the death of her uncle, King William IV. She reigned for over 63 years, until her death in 1901, making her the longest-serving British monarch in history. During her reign, Victoria was known for her strong sense of duty and her devotion to her family. She is also remembered for the many social, economic, and political changes that occurred during her reign, including the expansion of the British Empire and the Industrial Revolution.
24	C	The United Kingdom was among the first group of countries to sign the Convention in 1950. The Convention is a treaty that sets out the fundamental human rights that are to be protected and respected by all signatory states. It is considered to be a cornerstone of modern human rights law and has been ratified by virtually all countries in the world. The UK's decision to sign

the Convention reflects its commitment to upholding and protecting the human rights of its citizens and of people around the world.

Answers to Practice Test 3

	ANSWER	EXPLANATION
1	FALSE	The Commonwealth of Nations, also known as the Commonwealth, is a voluntary association of 54 countries that are largely former British colonies. Membership in the Commonwealth is open to any country that is willing to accept the values and principles of the organization, which include democracy, human rights, and the rule of law. Countries that choose to join the Commonwealth agree to work together in order to promote peace, prosperity, and cooperation among their member states.
2	B	In the criminal justice system of the United Kingdom, a jury is a group of individuals who are chosen to listen to the evidence presented at a trial and to reach a verdict based on that evidence. The jury's job is to determine whether the defendant is guilty or not guilty of the crime with which they have been charged. In Scotland, there is a third possible verdict: "not proven." This means that the jury was unable to reach a unanimous decision on the defendant's guilt, but did not

acquit them either. Instead, the case is considered to be "not proven," and the defendant is not punished.

3	C	The European Union (EU) was established on the basis of the Treaty of Rome, which was signed on March 25, 1957 by six western European countries: Belgium, France, Germany, Italy, Luxembourg, and the Netherlands. At the time, the organization was known as the European Economic Community (EEC). The EEC was created with the aim of promoting economic integration and cooperation among its member countries, and it eventually evolved into the EU, which has a much broader mandate and encompasses a wide range of policy areas.
4	A	The PDSA (People's Dispensary for Sick Animals) is an animal welfare charity based in the United Kingdom. The organization was founded in 1917 by Maria Dickin, a British philanthropist who was deeply concerned about the suffering of animals in the urban areas of London. Today, the PDSA provides a range of services to pets and their owners, including veterinary care, pet insurance, and pet adoption. The organization is funded through donations and is dedicated to improving the lives

of animals and promoting responsible pet ownership.

| 5 | FALSE | In the United Kingdom, arranged marriages, in which both parties willingly agree to the marriage, are generally considered to be acceptable. While the concept of arranged marriage may be unfamiliar or even controversial to some people in the UK, it is an important part of the culture and traditions of many communities, and it is recognized as a valid form of marriage by the law. In an arranged marriage, the parents or other family members of the couple typically play a central role in choosing the marriage partner, and both parties are expected to give their consent to the arrangement. As with any marriage, the happiness and well-being of the couple is of primary importance. |
| 6 | C | In the House of Commons, the party that holds the second largest number of seats is known as the opposition. The opposition is responsible for criticizing and scrutinizing the actions and policies of the government, which is typically led by the party that holds the most seats in the House of Commons other than the government. The opposition plays a critical role in the democratic process, as it helps to hold the |

government accountable and to ensure that it is working in the best interests of the people.

7   A   The Home Secretary is a cabinet minister in the United Kingdom who is responsible for overseeing the country's law enforcement agencies, including the police and the security services. The Home Secretary also has responsibility for immigration policy and for maintaining border control. In this role, the Home Secretary is responsible for ensuring the safety and security of the people of the United Kingdom and for managing the flow of people into and out of the country. The Home Secretary is a senior member of the government and plays a key role in shaping the country's policies on crime, policing, and immigration.

8   A, C & D   Income tax is a tax that is levied on an individual's income or on a company's profits. The money raised from income tax is used to fund a wide range of government services and initiatives, including infrastructure projects (such as roads and bridges), education, law enforcement, and the armed forces. These services are essential for the functioning of a modern society and are paid for by taxpayers through the income tax system.

9	TRUE	In the United Kingdom, it is illegal to be violent or abusive towards a partner, regardless of the victim's gender or the relationship status of the couple. This includes physical violence, as well as emotional, psychological, or financial abuse. Any individual who engages in such behavior can be prosecuted under the law. Domestic violence and abuse are serious crimes that have a profound impact on the victims and are not tolerated in any form. If you or someone you know is experiencing domestic violence, it is important to seek help and support as soon as possible. There are various resources available to assist victims of domestic violence, including shelters, hotlines, and counseling services.
10	TRUE	The Speaker of the House of Commons is a member of Parliament (MP) who is elected by their fellow MPs to preside over debates in the House of Commons. The Speaker is responsible for maintaining order in the House and ensuring that the rules of parliamentary procedure are followed. Although the Speaker is an MP and represents a constituency like any other MP, they are expected to be neutral and to refrain from expressing partisan views. This

means that the Speaker does not represent a political party and is not expected to advocate for any particular policy positions. Instead, the Speaker's primary role is to facilitate the work of the House of Commons and to ensure that all MPs have the opportunity to contribute to debates.

| 11 | B | Many elected representatives, including Members of Parliament (MPs), Members of the Welsh Assembly, Members of the Scottish Parliament (MSPs), and Members of the European Parliament (MEPs), hold regular "surgeries" in their local communities. Surgeries are sessions during which constituents can meet with their representative in person to discuss issues of concern to them. Surgeries provide an opportunity for individuals to voice their opinions, ask questions, and seek guidance or assistance on matters that are important to them. They are a useful way for elected representatives to stay in touch with the needs and concerns of the people they represent and to provide assistance when needed. |
| 12 | C | The Scottish Parliament is the devolved parliament of Scotland, which is a constituent country of the United Kingdom. The parliament is responsible for |

making decisions on a range of issues that affect the people of Scotland, including health, education, and the environment. The elected members of the Scottish Parliament, known as Members of the Scottish Parliament (MSPs), represent the people of Scotland and work to ensure that the country is governed in the best interests of its citizens. The Scottish Parliament meets in the Holyrood building in Edinburgh, which is the capital city of Scotland.

13	D	Tennis is a sport that has its roots in medieval Europe, but it was not until the late 19th century that the modern form of the game emerged. The modern game of tennis was developed in England, and the first lawn tennis club was established in the country in 1872. The game quickly gained popularity and spread to other parts of the world, becoming a major international sport. Today, tennis is played by millions of people around the world and is a prominent part of the international sporting calendar.
14	FALSE	The police force is a public service organization that is responsible for maintaining law and order and protecting the public from crime and other threats. Police officers are trained to serve and protect all

members of the community, regardless of their background or where they live. The role of the police is to ensure the safety and security of the people, and to enforce the laws of the country. Police officers work to prevent crime, to investigate crimes that have been committed, and to bring those who have broken the law to justice. The police force is a vital component of the criminal justice system and plays a critical role in keeping communities safe.

15   B

If you are arrested by the police in the United Kingdom, you will be taken to a police station for further questioning. Upon arrival at the police station, a police officer will inform you of the reason for your arrest and will read you your rights, which include the right to remain silent and the right to legal advice. It is important to exercise these rights and to seek legal advice as soon as possible, as this can help to protect your interests and ensure that you are treated fairly. You have the right to contact a solicitor, who can provide you with legal representation and advise you on your rights and options. It is also important to remember that you are innocent until proven guilty and that you have the right to a fair trial.

| 16 | D | The Conservative Party, also known as the Tory Party, is a political party in the United Kingdom. The party is officially called the Conservative and Unionist Party, as it is committed to preserving the unity of the United Kingdom and to upholding the principles of conservatism. The Conservative Party is one of the two major political parties in the UK, along with the Labour Party, and it has a long history of political involvement in the country. The party has traditionally been associated with support for free enterprise, individual responsibility, and a strong national defense, and it has held power for much of the time since the establishment of the modern parliamentary system in the UK. |
| 17 | C | The Chartists were a group of political reformers in the United Kingdom who campaigned for greater democracy and political equality during the late 1830s and 1840s. The Chartists called for a number of changes to the electoral system, including universal suffrage (the right to vote for all men), annual elections, equal representation for all regions, secret ballots, and the ability of any man to stand for election as a Member of |

Parliament (MP). They also called for MPs to be paid, as at the time only wealthy individuals were able to afford to serve in Parliament. The Chartists' demands were largely inspired by the principles of democracy and fairness, and their campaign played a significant role in shaping the political landscape of the UK.

18	C	Adolf Hitler was a German politician who rose to power in the 1930s as the leader of the Nazi Party. He was appointed as chancellor of Germany in 1933, following a series of electoral victories by the Nazi Party, and he quickly consolidated his power by suppressing opposition and dissent. Hitler ruled Germany absolutely until his death in April 1945, using a variety of methods to control the population, including propaganda, censorship, and repression. His regime was responsible for numerous atrocities, including the Holocaust, in which millions of Jews and other minority groups were murdered. Hitler's rule ended with Germany's defeat in World War II and his subsequent suicide.
19	D	The Speaker of the House of Commons is a member of Parliament (MP) who is elected by their fellow MPs to preside over

debates in the House of Commons. The Speaker is responsible for maintaining order in the House and ensuring that the rules of parliamentary procedure are followed. Although the Speaker is an MP and represents a constituency like any other MP, they are expected to be neutral and to refrain from expressing partisan views. This means that the Speaker does not represent a political party and is not expected to advocate for any particular policy positions. Instead, the Speaker's primary role is to facilitate the work of the House of Commons and to ensure that all MPs have the opportunity to contribute to debates.

20   A   The Laurence Olivier Awards, also known as the Oliviers, are annual awards presented to recognize excellence in professional theater in London. The awards are named after the British actor Sir Laurence Olivier, who was widely considered one of the greatest actors of his time. The Oliviers are presented in a variety of categories, including best director, best actor, and best actress, among others, and they honor outstanding achievements in theater across a range of genres. The awards ceremony takes place at a different venue in

London each year and is attended by members of the theater community and other industry professionals.

21	D	The Battle of Agincourt was a significant military engagement that took place during the Hundred Years' War between England and France in the early 15th century. The battle was fought on October 25, 1415, and it resulted in a decisive victory for the English army, which was led by King Henry V. Despite being vastly outnumbered by the French, the English were able to defeat their opponents through a combination of superior tactics and the use of the longbow, a powerful and accurate ranged weapon. The victory at Agincourt was a major turning point in the Hundred Years' War and helped to establish England as a major European power.
22	A	The First World War, also known as World War I, was a global conflict that took place from 1914 to 1918. The war involved the majority of the world's nations—including all of the great powers—eventually forming two opposing military alliances: the Allies and the Central Powers. The war resulted in the deaths of millions of people and caused widespread destruction. The

British Empire, which included the United Kingdom and its colonies, suffered more than 2 million casualties during the war, including both military personnel and civilians. The impact of the First World War was felt around the world and had long-lasting consequences for the international political landscape.

| 23 | B | The Black Death was a pandemic of the bubonic plague that swept through Europe in the 14th century, killing millions of people in a short period of time. The disease is believed to have originated in Asia and was transmitted to Europe through trade routes. It spread rapidly, killing as much as one third of the population in many areas, including England, Scotland, and Wales. The Black Death had a profound impact on European society, leading to significant social and economic changes, and it is considered one of the most devastating events in human history. |

24   B   The Magna Carta is a document that was signed in 1215 by King John of England. The document, which is also known as the Great Charter, established the principle that the king was subject to the law, just like any other person. The Magna Carta protected the rights

of the nobility and placed limits on the king's power to collect taxes and to make and change laws. It also established the principle that the government could not take a person's property or freedom without just cause and due process of law. The Magna Carta was an important step in the development of constitutional government and the rule of law, and it has had a lasting influence on legal systems around the world.

Answers to Practice Test 4

	ANSWER	EXPLANATION
1	B	The cabinet is a committee of senior government officials that is responsible for making important decisions about government policy and for advising the head of government, typically the prime minister. Cabinet meetings are usually held weekly and are chaired by the prime minister. At these meetings, cabinet members discuss and debate issues of national importance and make decisions about the direction of government policy. The cabinet plays a crucial role in the formulation and implementation of government policy, and it is responsible for ensuring that the government is working effectively to serve the needs of the people.
2	A	Emmeline Pankhurst was a prominent British suffragette who played a leading role in the women's suffrage movement in the United Kingdom. Pankhurst was born in 1858 and spent much of her life campaigning for women's right to vote. She founded the Women's Social and Political Union (WSPU) in 1903 and led numerous protests and

284

demonstrations in support of women's suffrage. Pankhurst's efforts helped to raise awareness of the issue and contributed to the eventual passage of the Representation of the People Act in 1918, which granted some women the right to vote. Pankhurst died in 1928.

| 3 | A | The police are a public service organization that is responsible for maintaining law and order and protecting the public from crime and other threats. Police officers are trained to serve and protect all members of the community, regardless of their background or where they live. The role of the police is to ensure the safety and security of the people, and to enforce the laws of the country. Police officers work to prevent crime, to investigate crimes that have been committed, and to bring those who have broken the law to justice. The police are a vital component of the criminal justice system and play a critical role in keeping communities safe. |
| 4 | TRUE | The 1960s were a decade of significant social and cultural change, marked by the emergence of a counterculture that challenged many traditional values and norms. The decade is often referred to as the "swinging sixties," reflecting the sense of |

energy and liberation that characterized the time. The 1960s saw significant growth in British fashion, cinema, and popular music, and these cultural developments had a profound influence on society. Many of the trends and movements that emerged during the 1960s, such as the youth culture and the civil rights movement, continue to shape our world today.

| 5 | A | In the United Kingdom, individuals are required to pay taxes on their income, which includes a variety of sources such as wages from paid employment, profits from self-employment, taxable benefits, pensions, and income from property, savings, and dividends. Taxes are used to fund the various services and programs provided by the government, including education, healthcare, defense, and infrastructure. The tax system in the UK is progressive, meaning that people with higher incomes pay a higher percentage of their income in taxes than those with lower incomes. The amount of tax that a person pays depends on their income level and other factors, such as whether they are married and whether they have children. |
| 6 | A | Henry VIII was the King of |

England from 1509 to 1547, he dies in Januarary. He was known for his tumultuous personal life, including his six marriages, and for his role in the English Reformation, which led to the Church of England breaking away from the authority of the Roman Catholic Church. Henry VIII was a strong-willed and ambitious ruler, and he played a significant role in shaping the history and politics of England during his reign. He died on January 28, 1547, at the age of 55.

| 7 | A | The European Union (EU) is a political and economic union of 27 European countries that was originally established in 1957 as the European Economic Community (EEC). The EU was founded by six western European countries: Belgium, France, Germany, Italy, Luxembourg, and the Netherlands. These countries signed the Treaty of Rome on March 25, 1957, which established the EEC and set the foundation for the creation of a single market among its member states. Over time, the EEC evolved into the EU, which has expanded to include additional member states and has developed a range of policies and initiatives in areas such as trade, environmental protection, and regional development. |

8	C	1952 was the year Queen Elizabeth II came to power at 25. She was the longest-serving current head of state in the world, and in 2012, she celebrated her Diamond Jubilee, marking 60 years of her reign. Throughout her time as queen, Elizabeth II has played a central role in the life of the country, serving as a symbol of unity and continuity.
9	A	"A rose by any other name would smell as sweet" is a famous line from William Shakespeare's play Romeo and Juliet. The line is spoken by Juliet, one of the main characters, in Act II, Scene 2 of the play, as she reflects on the fact that names are arbitrary and do not change the essence of a thing. The line is often cited as an example of the idea that the true nature of something is independent of its name, and it has become one of the most well-known and frequently quoted lines from Shakespeare's works.
10	D	The Industrial Revolution was a period of significant economic and social change that took place in Europe and North America in the 18th and 19th centuries. It was marked by the development of new technologies, such as the steam engine, and the growth of factories and mass production.

The Industrial Revolution had a profound impact on society, leading to the development of new forms of work, the growth of cities, and the emergence of a new middle class. Many scientific discoveries played a key role in the progress of the Industrial Revolution, including James Watt's work on steam power. Watt's development of the steam engine helped to power the growth of industry, leading to increased productivity and the expansion of trade.

11	A	The Harrier jump jet is a British aircraft that is known for its unique ability to take off and land vertically. It was developed in the latter half of the 20th century and has been used by a number of military forces around the world. The Harrier is a highly versatile aircraft that is capable of operating from a variety of surfaces, including land, sea, and aircraft carriers. Its vertical takeoff and landing (VTOL) capabilities make it particularly useful for operations in areas where traditional runway facilities are not available. The Harrier jump jet is considered a pioneering British invention and has made a significant contribution to the development of aviation technology.

| 12 | D | The Northern Ireland Assembly is the devolved legislature of Northern Ireland, which has responsibility for a range of policy areas, including health, education, and the environment. The Assembly is made up of 90 elected members, known as Members of the Legislative Assembly (MLAs). MLAs are elected to the Assembly through a form of proportional representation, which aims to ensure that the number of seats won by each party reflects the percentage of votes received. The Assembly is based in Belfast and meets regularly to debate and vote on issues of importance to the people of Northern Ireland. It plays a crucial role in shaping the policy and direction of the region and in representing the views of the public. |
| 13 | D | The Palace of Westminster is the seat of the UK Parliament, which consists of the House of Commons and the House of Lords. The palace is a historic and iconic building in London, known for its striking architecture and its importance as the center of the UK's democratic process. The entrance to the Palace of Westminster is free, and members of the public are welcome to visit and explore the |

building. There are a number of guided tours available, which offer an opportunity to learn more about the history and functions of Parliament, and to see some of the most famous and interesting parts of the palace, such as the House of Commons chamber and the Clock Tower, home of Big Ben.

14   A   The Scottish Parliament is the devolved national legislature of Scotland, which has responsibility for a range of policy areas, including health, education, and the environment. The Parliament is based in Edinburgh and is open to the public. If you are interested in visiting the Scottish Parliament, you can get information, book tickets, or arrange tours through the visitor services department. Visitor services can provide you with information about the Parliament and its functions, and can help you to plan your visit. They can also answer any questions you may have about the Parliament and its role in shaping the policy and direction of Scotland. The Scottish Parliament is an important and interesting place to visit, and a tour can provide an opportunity to learn more about the history and workings of the Scottish political system.

15   A   The Whigs and the Tories were two political parties that emerged in the United Kingdom during the 17th century. The Whigs were a political group that supported constitutional monarchy and opposed the absolute power of the monarchy. They were associated with the idea of parliamentary democracy and favored religious tolerance and freedom of speech. The Tories, on the other hand, were a political group that supported the absolute power of the monarchy and opposed parliamentary democracy. They were associated with the Anglican Church and favored a strong, centralized government. During the 17th century, the Whigs and the Tories were the two main political parties in Parliament, and they often clashed over a range of issues, including religion, foreign policy, and the role of the monarchy. Despite their differences, both parties played important roles in shaping the political landscape of the United Kingdom during this period.

16   D   Emmeline Pankhurst was a prominent suffragette and women's rights activist in the United Kingdom. Along with others who were frustrated by the slow progress of the women's

suffrage movement, Pankhurst founded the Women's Social and Political Union (WSPU) in 1903. The WSPU was an organization that used more radical and direct action tactics to campaign for women's suffrage, such as civil disobedience, protests, and the use of violence. The organization was known for its motto "Deeds not words," which reflected its belief that action was needed to achieve change, rather than just talking about it. The WSPU played a significant role in the fight for women's suffrage in the UK, and Pankhurst is remembered as a pioneering figure in the women's rights movement.

| 17 | B | The House of Commons is one of the two chambers of the UK Parliament, along with the House of Lords. The House of Commons is regarded as the more important of the two chambers because its members are democratically elected, while members of the House of Lords are either appointed or inherited their titles. The House of Commons is responsible for representing the interests and concerns of the people of the UK, and it plays a central role in the legislative process. Members of the House of Commons, known as Members of Parliament (MPs), are |

elected to represent specific constituencies, and they are responsible for representing the views of their constituents in Parliament. The House of Commons is also responsible for scrutinizing the work of the government and holding it accountable to the people of the UK.

18 D   The Scottish Exhibition and Conference Centre (SECC) is a large venue in Glasgow, Scotland, that is used for a range of events, including exhibitions, conferences, concerts, and other types of entertainment. The SECC is located on the banks of the River Clyde, in the Finnieston area of Glasgow. It comprises a number of different spaces, including an exhibition hall, conference facilities, and a large auditorium. The SECC is a popular and well-known venue in Glasgow, and it hosts a variety of events throughout the year. It is known for its modern facilities and convenient location, and it is a popular choice for organizers of events of all sizes.

19 B   As part of the process of becoming a British citizen, new citizens are required to participate in a citizenship ceremony. During the ceremony, they are required to swear or affirm loyalty to the

King and his successors. The oath or affirmation of allegiance is a formal declaration in which new citizens pledge to respect and uphold the laws and values of the UK, and to be a good citizen. The citizenship ceremony is an important step in the process of becoming a British citizen, and it is a symbolic moment in which new citizens formally commit to their new country. The ceremony is usually conducted by a local authority official, such as a mayor or a councilor, and it is usually attended by friends and family of the new citizen.

20   B   Before the 18th century, agriculture was the dominant industry in Britain, and it was the main source of employment for many people. During this period, most of the population lived in rural areas and worked in agriculture, either as farmers or as farm laborers. The agricultural sector was the primary source of food, fiber, and other raw materials for the UK, and it played a central role in the country's economy. The 18th century saw the beginning of the Industrial Revolution in Britain, which marked a shift away from agriculture and towards industrial production. The Industrial Revolution led to a growth in

manufacturing and other industries, and it changed the way people lived and worked in Britain. Despite this shift, agriculture remained an important part of the UK economy, and it continues to play a significant role to this day.

| 21 | A & C | In the UK, every citizen who is summoned to do jury service must serve unless they are not eligible or they provide a good reason to be excused. Eligibility for jury service is determined by a number of factors, including age, nationality, and criminal history. For example, individuals who have a criminal conviction may not be eligible to serve on a jury. In addition, individuals who are over a certain age, or who are not British citizens, may also be exempt from jury service. If an individual is summoned to do jury service but meets one of these exceptions, they may be excused from serving. However, if they are eligible and do not have a good reason to be excused, they are required to serve. Good reasons for being excused from jury service may include ill health or other personal circumstances that would make it difficult for an individual to serve. |
| 22 | C | The European Economic Community (EEC), which later |

became the European Union (EU), was formed in 1957 by six western European countries: West Germany, France, Belgium, Italy, Luxembourg, and the Netherlands. The EEC was created as a way to promote economic cooperation and integration among its member countries, and it was initially focused on the promotion of free trade and the creation of a common market. The UK initially did not wish to join the EEC, but it eventually decided to do so in 1973, along with Ireland and Denmark. The UK's decision to join the EEC was controversial, and it was the subject of much debate and discussion in the country. However, the UK ultimately became a member of the EEC, and it has remained a member of the EU since it was formed in 1993.

| 23 | B | The Prime Minister (PM) is the head of the UK government, and he or she is responsible for leading the country and representing it on the world stage. The PM is the leader of the political party that is in power, and he or she is appointed by the monarch on the advice of the House of Commons. As the leader of the government, the PM has a number of important duties and responsibilities. He or she |

appoints the members of the cabinet, which is a committee of senior government ministers who are responsible for specific policy areas. The PM also has the power to make many important public appointments, including judges, ambassadors, and other officials. The PM is also responsible for setting the direction of government policy, and he or she plays a central role in the legislative process.

24　C　During the Middle Ages many knights took part in the Crusades, in which European Christians fought for control of the Holy Land.

Answers to Practice Test 5

	ANSWER	EXPLANATION
1	A	The Scottish Parliament Building is the home of the Scottish Parliament at Holyrood, within the UNESCO World Heritage Site in central Edinburgh. The building was designed by the Spanish architect Enric Miralles and opened in 2004. It is located at the bottom of the Royal Mile, next to the Palace of Holyroodhouse.
2	B	The Northern Ireland Assembly is a devolved legislative body that has the power to make decisions on a wide range of issues that affect the people of Northern Ireland. It has the authority to legislate on matters such as education, agriculture, the environment, health and social services, and it is responsible for the administration of these policy areas within the region. However, the Assembly does not have the power to make decisions on defence or foreign affairs, as these are reserved to the UK government. The Assembly is located in Belfast, and it is made up of 90 elected members known as MLAs (Members of the Legislative Assembly). The

Assembly operates under a system of power-sharing, which means that decisions are made by consensus and all parties are represented in the government. This system was put in place to help promote stability and reconciliation in Northern Ireland after years of conflict.

3	B	The Man Booker Prize for Fiction is a prestigious literary award that has been given annually since 1968 to recognize the best novel written in English by an author from the Commonwealth, Ireland, or Zimbabwe. The prize is named after the financial services company Man Group, which sponsors the award, and it is considered one of the most prestigious literary prizes in the world. Past winners of the Man Booker Prize for Fiction include many notable authors such as Ian McEwan, Hilary Mantel, and Julian Barnes. The award is highly coveted by authors and is seen as a mark of excellence in the literary world. Each year, a panel of judges selects a shortlist of novels from a wide range of submissions, and the winner is chosen from this shortlist based on the quality of the writing, the originality of the ideas, and the overall impact of the book.

| 4 | B | There are three devolved administrations in the UK: the Welsh Assembly, the Scottish Parliament, and the Northern Ireland Assembly. Each of these administrations has its own legislative powers and is responsible for governing certain policy areas within its own region. The Welsh Assembly is located in Cardiff and has the power to legislate on matters such as education, health, and the environment. The Scottish Parliament is located in Edinburgh and has the authority to make laws on issues such as education, health, and justice. The Northern Ireland Assembly is based in Belfast and has the power to make decisions on matters such as education, agriculture, and the environment. These devolved administrations operate under a system of devolution, which allows them to make decisions that are best suited to the needs of their own regions. |
| 5 | B | Henry Purcell was a prominent English composer who was active in the late 17th century. He is widely regarded as one of the greatest composers in British history, and his work has had a lasting impact on the development of Western classical |

music. Purcell was born in London in 1659, and he began his musical career as a choirboy at Westminster Abbey. He later became the organist at the Abbey, and he composed a wide range of music for the church, including anthems, hymns, and service music. In addition to his work in the church, Purcell also composed operas and other secular music, and he is credited with developing a distinctively British style that was distinct from the styles of other European composers of the time. Purcell's music is known for its expressive melodies, rich harmonies, and innovative use of musical form, and it has had a lasting influence on composers of all genres.

6   D   In the United Kingdom, it is illegal to possess, use, or distribute certain drugs that are considered harmful to society. These drugs, which include substances such as heroin, cocaine, ecstasy, and cannabis, are classified as controlled substances under the Misuse of Drugs Act 1971. This legislation prohibits the possession, use, and distribution of these drugs and sets out penalties for those who are found to be in violation of the law. The illegal status of these drugs reflects the fact that they are

considered to have a high potential for abuse and can have serious negative effects on the health and well-being of individuals who use them. The UK government takes a strict approach to drug offenses and works to prevent the spread of drug use and abuse within the country.

7   A   In Scotland, there are several television channels that are dedicated to providing programming that is specifically tailored to the Scottish audience. These channels typically feature a mix of locally-produced content and programming from other sources, and they may also include programming that is produced in the Gaelic language. The Gaelic language is a Celtic language that is spoken by a small minority of people in Scotland, and there is a dedicated channel that broadcasts programming in Gaelic for those who speak the language. This channel is available to viewers throughout Scotland, and it offers a range of programming that is designed to reflect the culture, history, and traditions of the Gaelic-speaking community. Overall, the presence of these Scotland-specific channels and the availability of programming in

Gaelic reflects the diversity and cultural richness of Scotland and the importance of preserving and promoting these cultural traditions.

8   D   During the Industrial Revolution, which took place in the late 18th and early 19th centuries, many workers in the UK were subjected to extremely poor working conditions. At this time, there were few laws in place to protect the rights of employees, and many workers were forced to work long hours in dangerous and unhealthy environments. Children were often employed in these same conditions, and they were treated in the same way as adult workers, with no consideration given to their age or physical ability. Working conditions during the Industrial Revolution were characterized by low wages, hazardous conditions, and a lack of job security. Many workers were also required to work on Sundays, and there were no laws to protect their right to a day of rest. Overall, the Industrial Revolution marked a significant shift in the way work was organized and carried out in the UK, and it had a lasting impact on the lives and well-being of workers throughout the country.

9   C   Gustav Holst (1874-1934) was a

British composer who is best known for his orchestral suite The Planets, which was composed between 1914 and 1916. This work features seven movements, each of which is themed around one of the planets of the solar system. The Planets is one of Holst's most enduringly popular works and is considered a masterpiece of classical music. It has been widely performed and recorded by orchestras around the world and remains an important part of the classical repertoire. In addition to The Planets, Holst composed a number of other works in a range of different styles and genres, including operas, choral music, and instrumental pieces. He is widely respected as one of the most important and influential composers of the 20th century, and his contributions to classical music continue to be celebrated and remembered.

10   A   Proceedings in Parliament, which includes debates, committee meetings, and other official business, are open to the public and are also broadcast on television and radio. These broadcasts allow people to follow proceedings in Parliament from the comfort of their own homes or to catch up on proceedings that they may have missed. In

addition to being broadcast on television and radio, proceedings in Parliament are also published in official reports called Hansard. These reports provide a written record of what was said during debates and other proceedings in Parliament and are an important source of information for those interested in following the work of Parliament. Overall, the availability of television broadcasts and published reports like Hansard helps to increase transparency and accountability in the work of Parliament, and allows people to stay informed about the issues being debated and the decisions being made by their elected representatives.

11 A There are many large venues in the UK that host music events throughout the year, including Wembley Stadium and The O2 in Greenwich, south-east London. These venues are equipped with state-of-the-art facilities and can accommodate large crowds, making them popular choices for concerts and other music events. In addition to hosting concerts by some of the biggest names in music, these venues also host a variety of other events, including sports competitions, theatre performances, and conferences. With their convenient locations

and high-quality facilities, these venues are a vital part of the UK's cultural and entertainment scene and continue to attract millions of visitors each year.

12	A	The Killing Fields is a 1984 British-American historical drama film directed by Roland Joffé. The film is based on the true story of Cambodian journalist Dith Pran and his experience during the Cambodian genocide, which was perpetrated by the Khmer Rouge regime from 1975 to 1979. The film stars Sam Waterston as Sydney Schanberg, a New York Times journalist who was based in Cambodia during the genocide, and Haing S. Ngor as Dith Pran, his Cambodian interpreter and assistant. The film received widespread critical acclaim and was nominated for seven Academy Awards, including Best Picture and Best Director. It was a commercial success and is considered a classic of modern cinema.
13	B	Proceedings in Parliament, which include debates, statements, and other parliamentary business, are recorded and made available to the public in a number of ways. One way is through televised broadcasts, which can be accessed by individuals through their television service or online

through parliamentary websites. Additionally, written transcripts of parliamentary proceedings, known as Hansard, are published and can be found in physical copies at large libraries or accessed electronically through the website of the UK Parliament (www.parliament.uk). These written reports provide a permanent and accurate record of what was said and done in Parliament.

14	C & D	Inveraray Castle and Crathes Castle are two castles located in Scotland, a country in the northern part of the United Kingdom. Inveraray Castle is situated in the town of Inveraray in Argyll and Bute, while Crathes Castle is located in the town of Banchory in the Aberdeenshire region. Both castles are popular tourist attractions and offer visitors the opportunity to explore their grounds and learn about the history and culture of Scotland.
15	C	The Prime Minister, who is the leader of the government in the United Kingdom, has the authority to appoint a number of Members of Parliament (MPs) to serve as ministers in charge of various government departments. These ministers, who are typically among the most senior and experienced

MPs, are responsible for leading and managing their respective departments and implementing the policies and initiatives of the government. On average, the Prime Minister appoints around 20 MPs to serve as ministers.

16	C	Sir Charles (Charlie) Chaplin was a British actor, director, and producer who rose to fame in the early 20th century for his performances in silent films. One of his most iconic roles was that of the "Tramp," a character he developed and played in a number of films. Chaplin's talent, charisma, and comedic timing made him a beloved figure among moviegoers, and he quickly became one of the most famous actors of his time. In addition to his success in the British film industry, Chaplin also made a career in Hollywood, where he continued to act, direct, and produce a wide range of films.
17	B	According to data from the United Kingdom Office for National Statistics, the population of the UK as of 2010 was approximately 62 million people. This number represents the total number of individuals living within the UK, including citizens and non-citizens, and is based on estimates from the most recent

census conducted in that year.
The population of the UK has
continued to grow since 2010,
although at a slower rate, and as
of 2021, is estimated to be around
67 million people.

18 FALSE   The National Lottery is a form of
gambling in the United Kingdom
that involves the drawing of
numbers for cash prizes. It is
organized and operated by the
National Lottery Commission, a
public body that was established
by the UK government in 1994 to
oversee the running of the lottery.
The National Lottery is played by
purchasing a ticket with numbers
on it, and then participating in
weekly draws in which a set of
winning numbers is selected. If a
player's ticket matches the
winning numbers, they may be
eligible to receive a prize, which
can range in value from small
amounts of money to
multimillion-pound jackpots. The
National Lottery is a popular form
of entertainment in the UK, with
millions of people participating in
the weekly draws.

19 TRUE   Eid ul Adha, also known as the
Festival of Sacrifice, is an
important religious holiday
celebrated by Muslims around
the world. It is observed annually
on the 10th day of the month of
Dhul Hijjah, which is the final

month of the Islamic calendar. Eid ul Adha commemorates the story of Abraham and his willingness to sacrifice his son as an act of obedience to God. The holiday serves as a reminder to Muslims of their own commitment to their faith and to the principles of submission and obedience to God. It is a time for Muslims to come together with their families and communities to celebrate and give thanks for the blessings they have received.

20   C   Hanukkah, also known as the Festival of Lights, is a Jewish holiday that is celebrated annually for eight days and nights. It usually falls in November or December, depending on the Hebrew calendar. Hanukkah commemorates the miracle of the oil, which occurred during the Jewish revolt against the Greeks in the 2nd century BC. According to tradition, when the Jews rededicated the Temple in Jerusalem after defeating the Greeks, they found only enough oil to keep the menorah (a candelabra used in the Temple) lit for one day. However, the oil burned for eight days, which was enough time for them to prepare more. Hanukkah is a time for Jewish families to come together

and celebrate this miracle through the lighting of the menorah, the exchange of gifts, and the enjoyment of special foods.

21 B   Vaisakhi, also spelled Baisakhi, is a major Sikh festival that is celebrated on the 14th of April each year. It marks the founding of the Khalsa, a community of initiated Sikhs, and is considered one of the most important holidays in the Sikh faith. Vaisakhi is typically celebrated with parades, dancing, singing, and other festive activities. These celebrations are an opportunity for Sikhs to come together with their communities to honor their faith and heritage, and to reaffirm their commitment to living according to the principles of the Sikh religion. Vaisakhi is also a time for Sikhs to celebrate the abundance of the spring season and to give thanks for the blessings they have received.

22 D   Brief Encounter is a British film that was released in 1945. It was directed by David Lean, a British film director known for his work in both the British and American film industries. Brief Encounter is a classic romantic drama that tells the story of a woman (played by Celia Johnson) who falls in love with a married man (played by

Trevor Howard) while they are both on vacation. The film, which is set in the 1940s, is known for its powerful performances, its evocative music, and its realistic portrayal of love and longing. Brief Encounter is widely regarded as one of the greatest films of all time, and it continues to be admired and celebrated by audiences around the world.

23	B & C	Sailing and rowing are two popular activities in the United Kingdom that reflect the country's rich maritime heritage. Sailing involves the use of a boat or yacht to navigate through the water, and it can be enjoyed as a leisure activity or as a competitive sport. The UK has a long tradition of sailing, with a number of sailing clubs and regattas held throughout the country. Rowing, which involves propelling a boat using oars, is also popular in the UK, both as a recreational activity and as a competitive sport. Rowing is often associated with universities and schools, and there are a number of rowing clubs and regattas held in the UK. Both sailing and rowing continue to be enjoyed by people of all ages and abilities, and they are an important part of the UK's cultural identity.

24   C   According to data from the 2011
             Census of England and Wales,
             approximately 1.5% of the
             population identified as Hindu.
             This represents a significant
             minority within the population of
             England and Wales, and reflects
             the diversity of cultures and
             religions present in the UK. The
             Census is a comprehensive survey
             of the population that is
             conducted by the UK
             government every 10 years, and it
             provides valuable information
             about the demographics and
             characteristics of the population.
             The Census includes questions
             about a range of topics, including
             age, gender, ethnicity, religion,
             and employment, and the data
             collected is used to inform policy
             and decision-making at the
             national and local levels.

Answers to Practice Test 6

	ANSWER	EXPLANATION
1	B	Lancelot "Capability" Brown was an 18th-century English landscape architect who is known for his work in designing the grounds of country houses in a style that sought to make the landscape appear natural and unplanned. He was particularly skilled at creating gardens that featured grassy lawns, trees, and lakes, and he often worked with the architect Edwin Lutyens to design colorful gardens that complemented the houses he worked on. Brown's approach to landscape design was highly influential, and his work can be seen at many of the grand estates and gardens throughout the UK. His naturalistic style, which sought to blend the man-made with the natural, is still highly regarded and has inspired many other landscape designers.
2	D	According to the results of the 2009 Citizenship Survey, a comprehensive survey of the population of England and Wales conducted by the UK government, approximately 70% of people identified as Christian.

This was the largest proportion of any religion, followed by those who identified as Muslim (4%), Hindu (2%), Sikh (1%), and Jewish or Buddhist (both less than 0.5%). A small percentage of people (2%) identified as following another religion. The Citizenship Survey is a valuable source of information about the demographics and characteristics of the population, and it includes questions about a range of topics, including age, gender, ethnicity, religion, and employment. The data collected is used to inform policy and decision-making at the national and local levels.

3	B	The British Broadcasting Corporation (BBC) is a public service broadcaster that is funded by the money collected from TV licences. The BBC is responsible for providing television and radio programming to the public, and it is the largest broadcaster in the world in terms of both audience size and revenue. As a public service broadcaster, the BBC is independent of government and is funded through the money collected from TV licences, which is a mandatory fee that must be paid by households and businesses in the UK that own or

use a television. The BBC is responsible for producing a wide range of programming, including news, sports, entertainment, and children's programming, and it is known for its high standards of journalism and impartial reporting.

4	C	The Six Nations Championship is the most prestigious and well-known rugby union competition in the world. It is an annual event that features six teams: England, Ireland, Scotland, Wales, France, and Italy. These teams compete against each other in a round-robin tournament, with the team that accumulates the most points being crowned the champion. The Six Nations Championship is one of the oldest and most storied competitions in international rugby, and it is highly anticipated and followed by fans of the sport around the world. The competition is held every year, usually in the months of February and March, and it is an important event in the rugby calendar.
5	C	There are a number of poems that have survived from the Middle Ages, which is a period in European history that extends from the 5th to the 15th century. Some of the most famous and

well-known medieval poems include Chaucer's Canterbury Tales and Sir Gawain and the Green Knight. The Canterbury Tales is a collection of stories written by Geoffrey Chaucer, a 14th-century English poet, in which a group of pilgrims tell stories to each other on their way to Canterbury. Sir Gawain and the Green Knight is a poem about one of the knights at the court of King Arthur, and it is known for its complex narrative and use of symbolism. Both of these poems are widely studied and admired for their literary merit and historical importance.

6   FALSE   Eid al-Fitr, also known as the Festival of Breaking the Fast, is a major Muslim holiday that marks the end of the month of Ramadan. During Ramadan, Muslims observe a period of fasting from dawn until sunset, abstaining from food, drink, and other physical pleasures as a way of strengthening their spiritual discipline and devotion to God. Eid al-Fitr is the day when Muslims give thanks to Allah for giving them the strength and determination to complete the fast, and it is a time of celebration, feasting, and giving. Eid al-Fitr is an important event in the Islamic calendar, and it is

typically marked by special prayers, the giving of gifts, and the sharing of meals with friends and family.

7	C	Sir Walter Scott was a 19th-century Scottish poet and novelist who is known for his works that were inspired by Scotland and the traditional stories and songs of the border region between Scotland and England. Scott was born in Edinburgh and was deeply rooted in the culture and history of Scotland. He was particularly interested in the folklore and traditions of the Scottish Borders, and he drew on these sources for many of his poems and novels. Some of Scott's most famous works include his epic poems The Lay of the Last Minstrel and Marmion, as well as his novels Waverley and Ivanhoe, which are set in Scotland and are known for their vivid depiction of the landscape, culture, and history of the country. Scott's works have had a lasting impact on literature and continue to be widely read and admired.
8	B	One of the responsibilities shared by all those living in the UK is the obligation to treat others with fairness and respect. This principle is embedded in the laws and values of the UK, and it

is expected that all members of society will adhere to it. For individuals who are seeking permanent residence or citizenship in the UK, it is especially important to demonstrate a commitment to this principle, as it is considered an essential component of being a responsible and contributing member of the community. By treating others with fairness and respect, individuals can help to create a more inclusive and harmonious society, and they can play a role in upholding the values that are important to the UK.

9	A	Evelyn Waugh was a British novelist, writer, and journalist who is known for his satirical works, including Decline and Fall, Scoop, and Brideshead Revisited. Waugh was born in 1903 and was a prominent figure in the literary world of the mid-20th century. Her novels are known for their wit, humor, and social commentary, and they often explore themes of class, privilege, and moral decay.
10	D	The longest distance on the mainland of the United Kingdom is the journey from John O'Groats, a village on the north coast of Scotland, to Land's End, a promontory in the south-west

corner of England. This distance is approximately 870 miles, or 1,400 kilometers. The route from John O'Groats to Land's End is often described as the "end-to-end" journey, and it is a popular challenge for long-distance walkers, cyclists, and other adventurers. The journey takes travelers through a wide range of landscapes and environments, from the rugged coastlines and rolling hills of Scotland to the quaint villages and rolling countryside of England. The route is also rich in history and culture, with many landmarks and points of interest along the way.

| 11 | B | The £50 note is the highest denomination of banknote in circulation in the United Kingdom. It is issued by the Bank of England, the central bank of the UK, and is used as a means of payment for goods and services. The £50 note is the largest and most valuable of the banknotes currently in circulation in the UK, followed by the £20, £10, and £5 notes. The design of the £50 note changes from time to time, and it typically features a portrait of a well-known historical figure or important figure from the arts or sciences. The note is widely accepted as a form of payment |

and is used by people of all ages and walks of life.

12	A	Hogmanay is the Scottish term for the celebration of New Year's Eve, which is observed on the night of December 31st. In Scotland, Hogmanay is a major holiday that is often celebrated with much fanfare and enthusiasm. Many Scottish people consider Hogmanay to be a bigger holiday than Christmas, and they go to great lengths to mark the occasion with parties, feasts, and other festive activities. The celebration of Hogmanay typically includes the singing of traditional Scottish songs, the lighting of bonfires, and the participation in various rituals and customs. In Scotland, January 2nd is also a public holiday, and many people take the day off work or school to rest and recover from the celebrations of the previous night.
13	B	Snowdon is the highest mountain in Wales, and it is located in the Snowdonia National Park in the county of Gwynedd. Snowdon, which is also known as Yr Wyddfa in Welsh, stands at an elevation of 1,085 meters (3,560 feet) above sea level, and it is the highest peak in the British Isles outside of

Scotland. Snowdon is a popular destination for hikers and climbers, and it offers a range of challenging trails and routes that lead to the summit. The mountain is also a popular tourist attraction, with a narrow gauge railway that runs from the base to the summit. Snowdon is surrounded by stunning scenery and is home to a variety of wildlife, making it an ideal destination for outdoor enthusiasts and nature lovers.

14   B   Bobby Moore was an English football player who is best known for captaining the national team that won the World Cup in 1966. Moore was born in 1941 and began his career as a professional footballer at a young age. He played for a number of clubs throughout his career, including West Ham United, and he earned a reputation as one of the best defenders in the game. In 1966, Moore captained the English team at the World Cup, which was held in England. The team, which was led by Moore's solid and skillful play, went on to win the tournament, defeating West Germany in the final. Moore's contributions to the team's success made him a national hero, and he is remembered as one of the

greatest football players of all time. He passed away in 1993 at the age of 51.

15 B The National Trust is a charitable organization that was founded in 1895 by three volunteers: Octavia Hill, Sir Robert Hunter, and Canon Hardwicke Rawnsley. The National Trust is a conservation organization that works to protect and preserve the natural and cultural heritage of England, Wales, and Northern Ireland. The organization was founded with the goal of protecting and preserving the open spaces, historic buildings, and other landmarks that are important to the history and character of the UK. Today, the National Trust is one of the largest and most well-known conservation organizations in the world, and it is supported by a large membership base and a team of dedicated volunteers. The organization works to protect and care for a wide range of properties, including gardens, parks, woods, and coastlines, as well as historic houses and other buildings.

16 A, B & D During the 19th century, the United Kingdom was a major industrial powerhouse, and its industries led the world in a number of sectors. In particular,

the UK was a leading producer of iron, coal, and cotton cloth, and it accounted for more than half of the world's production of these commodities. The UK's industrial success was driven by a number of factors, including its abundance of natural resources, its skilled and innovative workforce, and its strong transportation and communication infrastructure. The country's industries, which included textiles, iron and steel, and coal and mining, were at the forefront of the Industrial Revolution, and they played a crucial role in the country's economic growth and development. The UK's industrial dominance waned in the 20th century, but it remains an important economic and technological power.

| 17 | FALSE | Bonfire Night, also known as Guy Fawkes Night, is a holiday that is celebrated annually in the United Kingdom on November 5th. The holiday commemorates the foiling of the Gunpowder Plot of 1605, in which a group of Catholics, led by Guy Fawkes, attempted to assassinate the Protestant King James I by blowing up the Houses of Parliament. The plot was discovered and foiled before it |

could be carried out, and Guy Fawkes was arrested and later executed for his involvement. Bonfire Night is marked with a variety of traditions and celebrations, including the lighting of bonfires, the setting off of fireworks, and the burning of effigies of Guy Fawkes. The holiday is an important part of British culture and is enjoyed by people of all ages.

| 18 | D | In Which We Serve, a 1942 film directed by David Lean and Noël Coward tells the story of a group of British sailors who are fighting in the war. The film, which was released during the height of the war, was widely praised for its emotional power and its depiction of the heroism and bravery of the British navy. It played an important role in boosting morale and helping to sustain support for the war effort. |
| 19 | TRUE | Your local council will contact you at your registered address to invite you to register on the electoral roll. The electoral roll is a list of eligible voters in a particular area, and it is used to determine who is eligible to vote in elections. To be eligible to vote in the UK, you must be a British, Irish, or Commonwealth citizen, and you must be over the age of 18. If you meet these |

requirements and you want to exercise your right to vote, you must register on the electoral roll. This can be done by contacting your local council, which will provide you with the necessary forms and information. Once you have registered, you will be added to the electoral roll, and you will be able to participate in elections and exercise your right to vote.

20   B   During the transatlantic slave trade, slaves were brought primarily from West Africa to the Americas, including the United States, the Caribbean, and South America. The transatlantic slave trade was a period in history that lasted from the 16th to the 19th century, during which millions of African men, women, and children were forcibly taken from their homes and transported to the Americas to work as slaves on plantations and in other industries. The majority of slaves came from West Africa, and they were captured and sold by European slave traders who operated out of coastal trading posts. Many of the slaves who were brought to the Americas came from present-day countries such as Senegal, Ghana, Angola, and Nigeria. The transatlantic slave trade was a brutal and

inhumane enterprise, and it had a profound and lasting impact on the African continent and the African diaspora.

| 21 | B, C & D | Governors and school boards play a critical role in raising school standards and improving the quality of education. They have three main responsibilities in this regard: setting the strategic direction of the school, ensuring accountability, and monitoring and evaluating school performance. In terms of setting the strategic direction of the school, governors and school boards work with the school leadership to develop and implement a vision and mission for the school, as well as goals and objectives that align with the school's values and priorities. They also help to create policies and procedures that support the school's efforts to improve student learning and achievement. To ensure accountability, governors and school boards oversee the financial and operational performance of the school, and they work to ensure that the school is meeting its legal and regulatory obligations. Finally, they monitor and evaluate school performance to identify areas for improvement and to track |

progress over time. By fulfilling these roles, governors and school boards help to create the conditions that enable schools to achieve high standards and provide a high-quality education for all students.

22   A & D   Recycling is an important activity that helps to conserve natural resources, reduce energy consumption, and minimize waste. By recycling as much of your waste as possible, you can help to protect the environment and support sustainable practices. When we recycle materials, we use them to make new products, which requires less energy than extracting raw materials from the earth. This means that we can reduce our reliance on non-renewable resources and lower our carbon footprint.

Recycling also helps to reduce the amount of rubbish that is created, which means that less waste is sent to landfill sites. Landfills are a major source of pollution and can have negative impacts on the environment and human health. By recycling, we can help to reduce the amount of waste that is sent to landfill and protect the environment for future generations.

23   D   The Super League is the most well-known rugby league club competition. Rugby league is a sport that is played with a ball and is similar to rugby union, but there are some key differences between the two sports. Rugby league is played with 13 players on each team, and the rules of the game allow for more continuous play and a faster pace of play than rugby union. The Super League is the top level of professional rugby league in the UK, and it is contested by clubs from England and France. The competition is organized by the Rugby Football League (RFL), the governing body for rugby league in the UK, and it is held annually. The Super League is known for its high-scoring matches and intense competition, and it attracts a large and passionate following of fans.

24   B   The Dame is a traditional character in British pantomimes, which are festive stage productions that are typically performed during the holiday season. The Dame is typically played by a man in drag, and she is known for her exaggerated costume, makeup, and mannerisms. The Dame is usually a comedic character and is

known for her bawdy humor and her ability to get laughs from the audience. She is often portrayed as a larger-than-life figure, and she is often the butt of jokes and pranks. The Dame is a beloved and enduring character in British pantomimes, and she is an important part of the tradition of these festive productions.

Answers to Practice Test 7

	ANSWER	EXPLANATION
1	C	Admiral Horatio Nelson was in charge of the British fleet at Trafalgar, and he is remembered as one of the greatest naval commanders in history. Nelson was killed in the battle, but his legacy lived on, and he was celebrated as a hero by the British people. Today, Nelson's Column in Trafalgar Square in London serves as a monument to his memory and his contributions to the nation.
2	A	Edmund Halley was an English astronomer and mathematician who made significant contributions to the fields of astronomy and mathematics. One of Halley's most notable achievements was his discovery of the periodic nature of comets. Halley noticed that the orbits of bright comets reported in 1531, 1607, and 1682 were similar, and he suggested that the trio was actually a single comet that was making periodic return trips through the solar system. Halley's hypothesis was groundbreaking, and it paved the way for the development of modern celestial mechanics. Halley's prediction

that the comet would return in 1758 was later proven to be correct, and the comet is now known as Halley's Comet in his honor. Halley's work was widely recognized in his time, and he is remembered as one of the most influential astronomers in history.

| 3 | D | Richard Austen Butler, later known as Lord Butler, was a British politician who served as a Member of Parliament (MP) for the Conservative Party. He was first elected to Parliament in 1923, and he went on to hold several positions within the party. In 1941, Butler was appointed as the Minister of Education, a position he held until 1945. As Minister of Education, Butler was responsible for overseeing the education system in England and Wales and implementing policies and initiatives to improve access to education and raise standards. He was widely respected for his knowledge and expertise in education policy, and he made significant contributions to the field during his time in office. After his tenure as Minister of Education, Butler went on to hold a number of other positions, including Chancellor of the Exchequer and Deputy Prime Minister. He was later made a life peer and took the title Lord |

Butler of Saffron Walden.

4	A, C & D	During the Victorian era, the British Empire experienced a period of rapid expansion, and it grew to encompass a vast territory that included much of India, Australia, and Africa. At its peak, the British Empire was the largest and most powerful empire in the world, and it controlled a quarter of the world's population and land area. The expansion of the British Empire during the Victorian period was driven by a number of factors, including economic interests, military power, and a belief in the superiority of British culture and values. The Victorian period was marked by a number of significant events and developments that shaped the course of the British Empire, including the colonization of India, the establishment of colonies in Australia, and the conquest of large parts of Africa. The legacy of the British Empire and the Victorian period remains an important and controversial aspect of British history.
5	D	There are several ways to contact Members of Parliament (MPs) in the UK. You can write to them or call them at their constituency office, or you can contact them at their office in the House of

Commons. The address of the House of Commons is: The House of Commons, Westminster, London SW1A OAA. The main telephone number for the House of Commons is 0207729 3000. In addition to these methods of communication, many MPs also hold regular local "surgeries" where constituents can meet with them in person to discuss issues that are of concern to them. These surgeries are typically held at a local office or community center, and they provide an opportunity for constituents to speak directly with their MP and raise any issues or concerns they may have.

6   A   Isaac Newton was an English scientist and mathematician who is widely considered to be one of the greatest scientists in history. He made significant contributions to a number of fields, including physics, mathematics, and astronomy, and his work laid the foundations for many of the scientific principles that we take for granted today. Newton was born in Lincolnshire, a county located in eastern England, in 1643. He grew up in a small village in Lincolnshire and received his early education at the King's School in Grantham, a town

located in the same county. Newton went on to study at the University of Cambridge, where he became interested in mathematics and physics and began to formulate many of the ideas that would later make him famous. His work had a profound impact on the scientific community and helped to shape our understanding of the natural world.

7	C	Notes (paper money): £5, £10, £20 and £50 The currency used in the United Kingdom is the pound sterling, which is abbreviated as GBP (Great Britain Pound) and symbolized by the £ sign. The pound is divided into 100 pence, and there are a variety of coins and notes in circulation. The denominations of coins in the UK include 1p, 2p, 5p, 10p, 20p, 50p, £1, and £2, while the denominations of notes (paper money) include £5, £10, £20, and £50. The currency of the UK is used for transactions and transactions throughout the country, and it is recognized as a strong and stable currency that is widely used around the world.
8	B	The United Kingdom originally decided not to join the European Union, a political and economic

organization that comprises 27 member states in Europe. However, in 1973, the UK changed its position and became a member of the EU. The UK remained a member of the EU for more than four decades, but in February 2020, it left the organization and officially ceased to be a member. The decision to leave the EU was the result of a referendum held in 2016 in which a majority of voters in the UK voted in favor of withdrawing from the EU. The UK's exit from the EU, commonly referred to as Brexit, has had significant implications for the country's political, economic, and social landscape, and it continues to be a major topic of debate and discussion in the UK and beyond.

9   D   Wilfred Owen and Siegfried Sassoon were two British poets who were deeply affected by their experiences in the First World War. Both men served as soldiers during the conflict, and they were inspired to write about their experiences in powerful and moving poetry. Owen and Sassoon were among a group of poets known as the "war poets," who wrote about the horrors and devastation of the war, as well as the bravery and sacrifice of the soldiers who

fought in it. Their work is considered to be some of the most powerful and poignant writing about the First World War, and it continues to be widely read and studied today. Owen and Sassoon's poetry provides a poignant and poignant insight into the human cost of the war and the devastating impact it had on the lives of those who experienced it.

| 10 | B & D | The 1930s was a decade marked by economic hardship and political turmoil, as the world struggled to recover from the effects of the Great Depression. Despite these challenges, the 1930s also saw the development of new industries in the UK, including the automobile and aviation sectors, which helped to provide some much-needed economic growth and job opportunities. Overall, the 1930s were a challenging and difficult period for the UK, but the country eventually emerged from the depression and went on to rebuild and prosper in the decades that followed. |

| 11 | D | Christmas is a widely celebrated holiday that is observed annually on December 25. It is a Christian festival that commemorates the |

birth of Jesus Christ, who is considered by many to be the son of God and the savior of humanity. Christmas is typically marked by a variety of religious and cultural traditions, including the exchange of gifts, the decorating of trees, and the singing of carols. Many people also attend church services on Christmas Day to celebrate the birth of Jesus and to give thanks for his teachings and sacrifice. In addition to its religious significance, Christmas is also a time of celebration and joy, and it is an important holiday for many people around the world.

12	D	The Bessemer process was an innovative method for the mass production of steel that was developed in the mid-19th century. It involved blowing air through molten iron to remove impurities, resulting in a high-quality, cost-effective steel that could be used in a variety of applications. The development of the Bessemer process had a major impact on the industrialization of the UK and other countries around the world, as it facilitated the growth of key industries such as shipbuilding and rail transportation. The ability to produce large quantities of steel at a low cost enabled the

construction of ships and railroads on a scale that was previously unimaginable, and these industries played a crucial role in the economic development of the UK and other countries. The Bessemer process remains an important part of the modern steel industry and continues to be used to produce steel for a variety of purposes.

13	TRUE	As of 2020, the higher education participation rate for young women in the UK has reached 56.6%, while the participation rate for young men is 44.1%. This represents a significant increase in the number of young women pursuing higher education compared to previous years, and it reflects the increasing importance of education in today's society. Higher education can provide young people with the skills and knowledge they need to succeed in their chosen careers, and it can also offer a wide range of personal and professional development opportunities. The higher education participation rates for young men and women are closely watched by policymakers and educators, as they provide insight into the state of education in the UK and the opportunities available to young people.

14	C	Bradford is a city located in the county of West Yorkshire, in the north of England. It is situated approximately 180 miles northwest of London, and it is the fourth-largest city in the UK. Bradford has a rich history and a diverse cultural heritage, and it is known for its industrial past and its thriving arts and cultural scene. The city is home to a number of famous landmarks, including the National Science and Media Museum, the Bradford Cathedral, and the Bradford Industrial Museum, which showcase the city's rich history and cultural heritage. Bradford is an important regional center and is a popular destination for tourists and visitors from around the UK and beyond.
15	D	Britain has a long and rich history of sports and athletics, and many popular sports that are played around the world today originated in the UK. Some of the most well-known sports that began in Britain include cricket, football (soccer), lawn tennis, golf, and rugby. These sports have a long and storied history in the UK, and they continue to be popular today, with millions of people participating in them and watching them as spectators. In addition to these sports, the UK is

also home to a number of other popular athletics, including athletics (track and field), boxing, and cycling, among others. The UK has a strong tradition of sports and athletics, and it is home to many world-class athletes and sporting events.

16   A   In the UK, it is a legal requirement for anyone who owns or uses a TV, computer, or other device that can be used to watch or record television programs to have a valid television license. A television license is a form of payment that is used to fund the British Broadcasting Corporation (BBC), which is a public service broadcaster that provides television and radio programs to the UK. The BBC is funded in part by the money collected from television licenses, which allows it to provide high-quality programming and services to the public. If you own or use a TV or other device that can be used to watch or record TV programs, you must have a valid television license in order to do so legally. Failure to have a television license when required can result in fines and other penalties.

17   TRUE   In the UK, girls on average tend to achieve higher academic qualifications than boys when

they leave school. This trend is reflected in the results of national exams and assessments, which consistently show that girls outperform boys in a number of subjects, including mathematics, science, and reading. The reasons for this gender gap in academic achievement are complex and multifaceted, and they may be influenced by a range of factors, including societal expectations, cultural influences, and individual differences. Despite this gender gap, both boys and girls have the potential to succeed academically, and it is important to provide all students with the support and resources they need to reach their full potential.

18   A & C   The Bessemer process was a revolutionary method for the mass production of steel that was developed in the mid-19th century. It involved blowing air through molten iron to remove impurities, resulting in a high-quality steel that could be produced at a lower cost than traditional methods. The development of the Bessemer process had a major impact on the industrialization of the UK and other countries around the world, as it facilitated the growth of key industries such as shipbuilding and rail

transportation.

19 C Sake Dean Mahomet was a British Indian entrepreneur and writer who was born in 1759 in the Bengal region of India. He grew up in India and received a traditional education in Islamic and Indian studies. Mahomet later moved to England, where he became a successful businessman and the proprietor of the Hindoostane Coffee House in London, the first Indian restaurant in the UK. In addition to his business pursuits, Mahomet was also a writer and published a number of works, including "The Travels of Dean Mahomet," an account of his experiences in India and England. Mahomet was an influential figure in his time and played a significant role in introducing Indian culture and cuisine to the UK.

20 A When seeking legal representation, it is important to carefully consider the qualifications and experience of the solicitor you are considering hiring. It is essential to find out what areas of law a solicitor specializes in and to ensure that they have the necessary expertise to effectively handle your case. This is especially important if you have a complex or specialized

legal issue, as you will want to work with a solicitor who has the skills and knowledge to navigate the specific legal challenges you are facing. Additionally, it is a good idea to check the solicitor's track record and to ask for references from past clients to get a sense of their reputation and the quality of their work. By doing your due diligence and carefully selecting a solicitor who is well-suited to your needs, you can increase your chances of achieving a successful outcome in your case.

| 21 | C | The United Kingdom (UK) is a sovereign country located off the northwest coast of Europe. It is made up of four constituent countries: England, Scotland, Wales, and Northern Ireland. The official name of the country is the United Kingdom of Great Britain and Northern Ireland, which reflects the fact that it is made up of Great Britain (which consists of England, Scotland, and Wales) and Northern Ireland. The UK has a long and storied history, and it is a diverse and culturally rich country with a thriving economy and a strong global influence. It is a parliamentary democracy, with a constitutional monarchy and a Westminster-style parliamentary system of government. The UK is |

a member of the United Nations and a number of other international organizations, and it is a major player in world affairs.

22	A	During their period of colonization, the Romans had a significant impact on the countries and territories that they controlled. They established a system of law and order, and introduced new plants and animals to the local environment. These actions had both positive and negative consequences, and they often had a lasting impact on the cultures and societies of the colonized regions.
23	A	The UK has a long history of producing world-renowned fashion designers, and the country is home to many talented and innovative designers who have made a significant impact on the global fashion industry. Some of the leading fashion designers of recent years in the UK include Mary Quant, Alexander McQueen, and the late Vivienne Westwood. These designers are known for their unique and creative designs, and they have helped to define the look and style of modern fashion. Each of these designers has made a name for themselves in the fashion industry, and they have contributed significantly to

the global fashion scene. Whether through their cutting-edge designs, their use of innovative materials, or their unique aesthetic vision, these designers have helped to shape the world of fashion and set the trends for future generations.

24 C   The development of architecture and design has always been an important part of the cultural landscape of the UK. Alongside the creation of buildings and structures, garden design and landscaping have also played a significant role in shaping the country's built environment. From the formal gardens of the grand estates of the aristocracy to the more modest gardens of middle-class homes, gardens have long been an important feature of the UK's landscape. Similarly, the art of landscaping has played a key role in shaping the country's public spaces, from the green spaces of cities to the rolling hills of the countryside. Whether through the creation of beautiful gardens and parks or the careful design of public spaces, the art of garden design and landscaping has had a major impact on the character and appearance of the UK.

Answers to Practice Test 8

	ANSWER	EXPLANATION
1	B	Sir Terence Conran was a renowned British interior designer and business magnate who made a significant impact on the world of design during the 20th century. Born in 1931, Conran was a pioneer in the field of interior design, and he played a key role in shaping the modern aesthetic of the post-war period. He was known for his innovative and practical approach to design, and he was instrumental in introducing many of the design ideas and trends that have become widely popular in the UK and beyond. Conran was also a successful entrepreneur and founded a number of successful design-related businesses, including the Conran Shop, Habitat, and the Design Museum. Despite his many professional accomplishments, Conran remained a down-to-earth and approachable figure, and he was widely admired and respected within the design community.
2	A	Thomas Chippendale was a renowned British furniture designer and maker who is widely considered to be one of the greatest designers of his time.

Born in 1718, Chippendale was active during the 18th century, a period that saw significant growth and development in the field of furniture design. He is best known for his contributions to the neoclassical style, which was characterized by a focus on symmetry, balance, and order. Chippendale's furniture was highly sought after by the wealthy and powerful of his time, and his work has continued to be highly regarded and collected by furniture enthusiasts around the world. In addition to his many accomplishments as a designer and maker,

| 3 | A | In addition to the various political parties and government bodies that play a role in shaping the political landscape of the UK, there are also a number of representative organizations that have an important influence on the country's political and economic policy. One such organization is the Confederation of British Industry (CBI), which is a membership organization that represents the views of British business and promotes the interests of its members. The CBI is made up of over 190,000 businesses, including small and medium-sized enterprises as well as large multinational |

corporations, and it plays a key role in shaping government policy and advocating for the interests of the business community. Other representative organizations that play an important role in the UK's political landscape include trade unions, which represent the interests of workers, and professional bodies, which represent the interests of specific professions or industries. Together, these organizations help to ensure that the voices and concerns of different groups within society are heard and taken into account by policymakers.

4   B   The United Kingdom is a diverse and multicultural society, with a rich and varied cultural heritage. Despite this diversity, there are certain shared values and responsibilities that are held in common by people of all backgrounds and cultures. These shared values and responsibilities include a commitment to democracy and the rule of law, respect for human rights and equality, and a sense of community and social responsibility. These values are reflected in the country's laws and institutions, and they form an important part of what it means to be a citizen of the UK. By

upholding these values and assuming the responsibilities that come with them, people from all walks of life can contribute to building a stronger, more united, and more prosperous society for everyone.

| 5 | A | Obtaining British citizenship or obtaining the right to settle in the UK can be a significant and rewarding experience, offering a range of opportunities and benefits. At the same time, however, it also brings with it certain responsibilities and obligations. For example, as a British citizen or resident, you are expected to respect the laws and institutions of the UK, to contribute to your community and to participate in the democratic process. You may also be expected to fulfill certain duties, such as serving on a jury or registering for military service if required. By fulfilling these responsibilities and taking advantage of the opportunities that come with living in the UK, you can make the most of your experience in this country and contribute to its success and prosperity. |
| 6 | A | Terrorist groups often seek to radicalize and recruit individuals to join their cause, often using various tactics and strategies to |

do so. These tactics can include the use of propaganda, social media, and other forms of communication to spread their message and appeal to potential recruits. Terrorist groups may also use various forms of manipulation and coercion to recruit people, including by exploiting vulnerabilities, offering financial incentives, or using violence and intimidation. In some cases, terrorist groups may even target specific groups or communities in their recruitment efforts, seeking to exploit social or political tensions in order to gain new members. It is important to be aware of these tactics and to be vigilant in order to prevent radicalization and recruitment by terrorist groups.

| 7 | A | The United Kingdom faces a variety of terrorist threats, both from domestic and international sources. The most serious of these threats is typically considered to be from Al Qaeda and its affiliates and other like-minded organizations, which have been responsible for a number of high-profile attacks in the UK and around the world. Other significant threats may include those posed by other extremist groups, both domestic and international, as well as lone |

actors or small cells who may be motivated by a range of ideological or personal grievances. In order to mitigate these threats and protect the UK and its citizens, the country has robust counter-terrorism measures in place, including intelligence gathering, law enforcement, and diplomatic efforts, as well as efforts to counter radicalization and prevent the recruitment of new terrorists.

8 B Individual electoral registration (IER) is a system in which each individual is responsible for registering themselves to vote, rather than one member of a household registering all members. This is in contrast to the previous system in Northern Ireland, known as household registration, where the head of the household was responsible for registering all eligible residents at the address.

9 A If you are unsure which local authority you fall under, you can use the website www.aboutmyvote.co.uk to determine your jurisdiction. Simply enter your postcode on the website and it will provide you with information about your local authority and other voting-related information. Alternatively, you can

also contact your local council or election officials directly for information about your local authority and how to register to vote. It is important to note that in order to be able to participate in elections, you must be registered to vote and meet all other eligibility requirements. By ensuring that you are registered and informed about the voting process, you can help to ensure that your voice is heard and that you are able to participate in the democratic process.

10   C   The electoral register is a list of individuals who are eligible to vote in elections and referendums. In order to ensure that the register is up to date and accurate, it is updated on an annual basis. The exact timing of the update can vary, but it typically occurs in September or October of each year. This allows any changes in eligibility, such as new residents moving into an area or citizens reaching the legal voting age, to be reflected in the register in time for the next election. The updated register is then used to compile the list of registered voters for polling stations, postal votes, and other electoral purposes.

11   A   In the UK, the laws governing radio and television coverage of

political parties and their activities require that a balanced and fair representation of rival viewpoints be maintained. This means that broadcasters must ensure that the airtime or coverage given to each political party is equal, and that no party is given preferential treatment. This requirement for balance and fairness is intended to prevent the manipulation of public opinion through the disproportionate exposure of certain viewpoints or parties, and to ensure that the electorate has access to a diverse range of perspectives when making informed decisions about their vote. In order to comply with these laws, broadcasters may need to carefully plan their coverage and allocate equal time to each party or candidate.

12   B   At the turn of the 19th century, the political system of Britain was significantly different from the democratic system that exists in the country today. At that time, the franchise (the right to vote) was limited to a small portion of the population, and the government was not elected by the people but rather appointed by the monarch or inherited through noble birth. This meant that the vast majority of the population had no say in the

decisions that affected their lives and were not able to participate in the political process. It wasn't until the introduction of reforms in the following decades, such as the Great Reform Act of 1832 and the Representation of the People Acts of the late 19th and early 20th centuries, that the franchise was gradually expanded and the foundations of modern democracy in Britain were established.

13   B   The Chartist movement was a political campaign that took place in Britain during the 1830s, 1840s, and 1850s, which aimed to bring about political and social reforms through the use of mass petitioning and other forms of civil disobedience. The Chartists sought to secure the right to vote for all men, to extend the franchise to include working-class men, and to introduce other democratic reforms such as secret ballots and the abolition of property qualifications for members of Parliament. Despite their efforts, the Chartist movement ultimately did not achieve many of its goals, and the reforms that they campaigned for were generally seen as having failed.

14   A   The franchise, also known as the right to vote, refers to the group

of people who are eligible to participate in the political process by casting a vote in elections and referendums. The franchise is an important aspect of democracy, as it determines who is able to have a say in the decisions that affect the country and its citizens. The qualifications for the franchise can vary from place to place and have changed over time. In the past, the franchise was often limited to a small portion of the population, such as property owners or men of a certain social class or race. In modern democracies, the franchise is generally extended to all adult citizens, although there may be some restrictions or disqualifications in place, such as a criminal record or lack of mental capacity.

| 15 | D | The third reform that the chartists demanded was for all regions to be equal in the electoral system. |
| 16 | C | Representation of the People Act of 1918 Act granted the right to vote to women over the age of 30 who met certain property qualifications, as well as to men over the age of 21 who had served in the military during World War I. However, this extension of the franchise did not apply to all women or all men, and many groups were still excluded from |

the political process. It wasn't until the Representation of the People Act of 1928 that the franchise was further extended to include all women and men over the age of 21, regardless of property qualifications. This act marked a significant step towards universal suffrage (the right to vote for all adult citizens) in Britain.

| 17 | B | Irish Gaelic, also known as Irish or Gaelic, is a Celtic language that is spoken by a minority of people in Northern Ireland, as well as in the Republic of Ireland and other parts of the world. Irish is one of the official languages of the Republic of Ireland and is recognized as an official language in Northern Ireland under the European Charter for Regional or Minority Languages. In Northern Ireland, Irish is spoken as a first language by a small percentage of the population, primarily in areas with a strong Irish cultural identity such as the Gaeltacht (Irish-speaking regions). |

| 18 | B | "Lawrence of Arabia" is a classic film that was released in 1962 and directed by David Lean. The film tells the story of T.E. Lawrence, a British military officer and diplomat who played a key role in the Arab Revolt against the Ottoman Empire during World |

War I. "Lawrence of Arabia" was a major critical and commercial success upon its release and has since become a classic of cinema. The film was directed by David Lean, a renowned British filmmaker known for his epic historical dramas such as "Doctor Zhivago" and "A Passage to India." "Lawrence of Arabia" was released in 1962 and was nominated for ten Academy Awards, winning seven, including Best Picture, Best Director for David Lean, and Best Actor for Peter O'Toole, who played the title role of T.E. Lawrence.

| 19 | B | In a survey of the religious affiliation of the population of a certain region, a significantly larger proportion of people identified as Christian (the majority religion), while much smaller proportions identified as belonging to other religions. Specifically, 4% of respondents identified as Muslim, 2% identified as Hindu, 1% identified as Sikh, less than 0.5% identified as Jewish or Buddhist, and 2% identified as following another religion. These percentages demonstrate the religious diversity of the region and highlight the fact that while Christianity is the dominant religion, there are also significant numbers of people belonging to |

other faiths.

20 C   According to the latest estimates, Christianity is the largest religion in the United Kingdom, with approximately 59% of the population identifying as Christian. There are a number of different denominations of Christianity present in the UK, including the Church of England, the Roman Catholic Church, Presbyterianism, and Methodism, among others. While Christianity is the majority religion in the UK, there is also a significant minority of people who practice other faiths, such as Islam, Hinduism, Judaism, and Buddhism. In addition, a significant proportion of the population identifies as non-religious or atheist. The religious landscape of the UK is diverse and multifaceted, with people belonging to a wide range of belief systems and traditions.

21 D   In the United Kingdom, individuals have the right to practice their chosen religion or to choose not to follow any religion at all. This freedom is protected by law, ensuring that individuals have the ability to freely express and exercise their religious beliefs without fear of persecution or discrimination.

22 D   The United Kingdom is home to a diverse array of religious

communities, each of which has established places of worship throughout the country. These religious buildings include Islamic mosques, Hindu temples, Jewish synagogues, Sikh gurdwaras, and Buddhist temples, among others. These structures serve as important centers for the practice of different religions and as hubs for the respective religious communities.

| 23 | A | The United Kingdom offers a wide range of shopping destinations for both residents and visitors. Many towns and cities feature a central shopping district, commonly referred to as the town center, which is home to a variety of stores, boutiques, and other retail establishments. In addition to these traditional shopping areas, the UK also boasts a number of large shopping malls and outdoor retail centers. Whether you're looking for high-end fashion, unique gifts, or everyday essentials, you'll find it all in the UK. |

| 24 | A | The inventor of the World Wide Web, Sir Tim Berners-Lee (1955-), is British. Information was successfully transferred via the web for the first time on 25 December 1990. |

Answers to Practice Test 9

	ANSWER	EXPLANATION
1	D	Mathematical Principle of Natural Philosophy by Isaac Netwon is one of the most renowned published works of his career was Philosophiae Naturalis Principia Mathematica (commonly translated as "Mathematical Principles of Natural Philosophy"). This influential text has had a lasting impact on the field of science and is widely considered a masterpiece.
2	B	Sir Isaac Newton was a renowned member of the Royal Society, one of the oldest scientific societies in the world. He was among the earliest members of this prestigious organization and made significant contributions to the fields of mathematics and physics throughout his career.
3	B	Sir Isaac Newton made the groundbreaking discovery that white light is composed of the colors of the rainbow. This insight, which he arrived at through his experimentation with prisms, helped to lay the foundations for the modern understanding of light and color.

4	D	It is strictly prohibited for police officers to abuse their authority, make false statements, behave rudely or abusively, or engage in racial discrimination. These behaviors are not only unprofessional and unethical, but they can also undermine trust in the police force and erode the public's confidence in the justice system.
5	B	Police and Crime Commissioners (PCCs) are responsible for setting local police priorities, allocating the local policing budget, and appointing the local Chief Constable. In this way, PCCs play a vital role in shaping the direction and focus of policing in their communities and ensuring that the needs and concerns of local residents are taken into account.
6	C	The police forces in the United Kingdom are organized into a number of separate agencies, each headed by a Chief Constable. These agencies are independent of the government and operate autonomously in carrying out their duties. This structure is intended to ensure that the police are accountable to the communities they serve and can effectively respond to local needs and concerns.

7	A	If you are arrested and taken to a police station, the arresting officer must inform you of the reason for your arrest. You also have the right to seek legal advice at this time. It is important to remember that you have rights even when you are under arrest and that you should not hesitate to assert them if you feel that they are being violated.
8	A	If a voter is unable to physically make it to a polling station or polling place due to difficulty with transportation or other circumstances, they can register to receive a postal ballot. This allows them to cast their vote by mail, ensuring that they can participate in elections even if they are unable to go to the polls in person.
9	D	In addition to providing their name and address, voters in Northern Ireland will also be required to present photographic identification when casting their ballot. This additional step is intended to help ensure the integrity of the electoral process and prevent fraud.
10	C	Initially, the United Kingdom was hesitant to join the European Economic Community (EEC), but it eventually became a member in 1973. This decision marked a significant shift in the country's foreign policy and marked the

beginning of its close relationship with the European Union.

11	A	In the United Kingdom, it is illegal to operate a motor vehicle without a valid insurance policy. Driving without insurance is considered a serious criminal offense and can result in significant fines, points on your driver's license, and even imprisonment in severe cases. It is important to always make sure you have a valid insurance policy before getting behind the wheel.
12	C	The acronym "EEC" stands for "European Economic Community". This organization, which was founded in the 1950s, was a precursor to the modern European Union and was established to promote economic cooperation among its member states.
13	A	British diplomats and lawyers played a crucial role in the drafting of the European Convention on Human Rights and Fundamental Freedoms, which was developed in the United Kingdom. This influential treaty, which was adopted in 1950, established a set of fundamental rights and freedoms that are protected in countries throughout Europe. It has had a significant impact on the legal systems of its member states and has helped to ensure that all individuals are treated

with dignity and respect.

14	A	The legal system in the United Kingdom can be broadly divided into two main categories: criminal law and civil law. Criminal law deals with offenses that are considered harmful to society as a whole and are punishable by the state, while civil law deals with disputes between individuals or organizations and is concerned with providing remedies for harm or injustice. Understanding the distinction between these two areas of law is important for anyone navigating the UK legal system.
15	A	Criminal law pertains to offenses that are considered harmful to society as a whole and are punishable by the state. These crimes are typically investigated by the police or another authority, such as a local council, and are tried in criminal courts. If an individual is found guilty of a criminal offense, they may face a range of penalties, including fines, imprisonment, or community service.
16	D	In the United Kingdom, it is illegal to sell or buy drugs such as heroin, cocaine, ecstasy, and cannabis. These substances are classified as controlled substances and their possession, distribution, and use are strictly regulated by law.

Breaking these laws can result in significant fines and imprisonment. It is important to be aware of the laws regarding controlled substances and to avoid engaging in illegal drug-related activities.

17   C   In 1932, John Logie Baird, a Scottish inventor, successfully transmitted the first television broadcast between London and Glasgow. This pioneering achievement marked the birth of television as we know it and paved the way for the development of the modern television industry. Baird's work has had a lasting impact on the way we communicate and access information and entertainment, and he is widely recognized as a pioneer in the field of telecommunications.

18   B   The acronym "IVF" stands for "in-vitro fertilization", a therapy used to treat infertility. This procedure, which was pioneered in the United Kingdom by physiologist Sir Robert Edward and gynaecologist Patrick Steptoe, involves the fertilization of an egg outside of the body and the subsequent transfer of the embryo back into the womb. IVF has helped countless individuals and couples become parents and has revolutionized the field of

reproductive medicine.

19	B	During the 1970s, the prices of goods and raw materials experienced a significant increase and the exchange rate between the pound and other currencies became unstable. This period of economic turmoil was characterized by rising inflation and fluctuating currency values, which had a significant impact on businesses and consumers alike.
20	B	The 1970s saw a spate of strikes across a number of industries and services, leading to tension between trade unions and the government. These strikes, which were often characterized by heated negotiations and disputes over working conditions and pay, had a disruptive effect on businesses and the economy as a whole. They also highlighted the complex relationship between labor and management and the ongoing struggle for workers' rights.
21	B	In the late 1970s, the post-war economic boom came to an end. Prices of goods and raw materials began to rise sharply and the exchange rate between the pound and other currencies was unstable. This caused problems with the 'balance of payments': imports of goods were valued at more than the price paid for

exports.

22	A	From 1970 through 1972 an explosion of political violence occurred in Northern Ireland. The deadliest attack in the early 70s was the McGurk's Bar bombing by the UVF in 1971. The violence peaked in 1972, when nearly 500 people, just over half of them civilians, were killed, the worst year in the entire conflict.
23	D	In 1972, the Northern Ireland Parliament was suspended and Northern Ireland was directly ruled by the UK government.
24	B	The task of rebuilding Britain after the devastation of the Second World War was a significant challenge for the British government. The war had caused widespread destruction and disrupted the country's economy and infrastructure, and it was up to the government to lead the rebuilding effort and restore stability to the nation. This was a monumental undertaking that required the mobilization of resources and the implementation of bold policies and initiatives. Despite the many challenges, the government was ultimately successful in rebuilding Britain and laying the foundations for a more prosperous and secure future.

Answers to Practice Test 10

	ANSWER	EXPLANATION
1	B	In the 1950s, the rebuilding process in the United Kingdom was hampered by a shortage of labor, and the government encouraged further immigration for economic reasons. Many industries, particularly those that were involved in the rebuilding effort, advertised for workers from overseas. This influx of immigrants helped to fill the labor gap and contributed to the rebuilding and recovery of the country.
2	A	One of the challenges facing the United Kingdom in the aftermath of World War II was a shortage of labor to help rebuild the country. This problem persisted into the 1950s and required the government to look for ways to address it. This included encouraging immigration and promoting industries that were involved in the rebuilding effort. Despite these challenges, the government was ultimately successful in rebuilding Britain and restoring stability to the nation.
3	B	"Do Not Go Gentle into That Good Night," a poem by Dylan Thomas,

was written in 1952 for the poet's dying father. This powerful and moving piece has become one of Thomas's most famous works and has been widely anthologized and adapted in various media. It is a testament to the enduring bond between father and son and a celebration of the human spirit's refusal to accept defeat.

| 4 | D | During the First World War, the Central Powers were a coalition of countries that included Germany, the Austro-Hungarian Empire, the Ottoman Empire, and later Bulgaria. These powers were opposed by the Allied Powers, which consisted of a diverse group of countries including France, the United Kingdom, and the United States, among others. The conflict between the Central Powers and the Allied Powers was a global war that lasted from 1914 to 1918 and had far-reaching consequences for the world. |
| 5 | D | The early twentieth century was marked by a major global conflict between several European nations, known as the First World War. This devastating war brought an end to the era of optimism and progress in Britain and had far-reaching consequences for the country and the world. The war, which lasted from 1914 to 1918, was one |

of the deadliest in human history and had a profound impact on the course of world events.

6	B	"Don't Look Now," a film directed by Nicolas Roeg, was released in 1973. This psychological thriller, which is based on a short story by Daphne du Maurier, is known for its innovative use of editing and its unsettling atmosphere. It has been widely praised by critics and has gained a cult following over the years.
7	B	"Touching the Void," a film directed by Kevin MacDonald, was released in 2003. This documentary tells the story of two mountaineers who are stranded on a mountain in the Peruvian Andes after one of them suffers a serious injury. It is based on a bestselling book of the same name and has been praised for its portrayal of the climbers' struggle for survival against seemingly insurmountable odds.
8	D	"Four Weddings and a Funeral," a film directed by Mike Newell, was released in 1994. This romantic comedy, which stars Hugh Grant and Andie MacDowell, follows a group of friends as they navigate the ups and downs of love and relationships. The film was a critical and commercial success and has become a modern classic.

9	C	By the end of 2014, international forces had assumed full responsibility for security in all provinces of Afghanistan. This marked an important milestone in the country's efforts to rebuild and stabilize after years of conflict. It also signaled a shift in the role of international forces, which had previously been responsible for providing support and assistance to Afghan security forces but were now fully responsible for maintaining order and protecting civilians.
10	B	The Iraqi invasion of Kuwait occurred in 1990. This military conflict, which was led by Iraqi dictator Saddam Hussein, resulted in the occupation of Kuwait by Iraqi forces and led to a major international crisis. The invasion was met with widespread condemnation and ultimately led to the deployment of a large international coalition, including forces from the United States, to liberate Kuwait and restore its sovereignty. The conflict had far-reaching consequences for the region and the world, and its legacy is still felt today.
11	C	British combat troops withdrew from Iraq in 2009, marking the end of a controversial military intervention that had lasted for

several years. The decision to pull out troops was the result of negotiations between the British government and the Iraqi authorities and reflected a shift in the country's security landscape. While the withdrawal of British troops was welcomed by many, it also raised questions about the long-term stability and security of Iraq, and its ability to maintain peace and order without the support of international forces.

12   A   The International Security Assistance Force (ISAF) is an international military organization that has been working to ensure that Afghanistan is no longer used as a safe haven for international terrorism. This includes efforts to prevent groups such as Al Qaeda from using Afghan territory to plan attacks on the international community. By providing security and stability in Afghanistan, ISAF aims to prevent the country from becoming a breeding ground for terrorism and to protect the international community from threats emanating from this volatile region.

13   A   The United Kingdom was one of the first countries to sign the European Convention on Human Rights in 1950, demonstrating its commitment to the protection of

fundamental rights and freedoms. This influential treaty, which has been ratified by all member states of the Council of Europe, establishes a set of standards for the protection of human rights and is an important part of the legal landscape in the UK and throughout Europe. The UK has played a leading role in the development and implementation of the Convention and has helped to ensure that it remains a cornerstone of human rights protection in Europe.

14 B Since the year 2000, the British armed forces have been actively involved in the global fight against international terrorism and the proliferation of weapons of mass destruction. This has included participation in military operations in Afghanistan and Iraq, as well as other efforts to promote security and stability around the world. The UK has played a key role in these efforts, using its military capabilities and expertise to help protect the international community from the threat of terrorism and the spread of dangerous weapons.

15 A Employment law is a branch of law that deals with disputes and issues that arise in the workplace, including matters related to

wages, unfair dismissal, and discrimination. It is designed to protect the rights of employees and ensure that they are treated fairly and with respect in the workplace. Employment law sets out the legal framework for the relationship between employers and employees and helps to ensure that the rights of both parties are respected and upheld.

16   B   You can learn more about the different types of crime in the United Kingdom by visiting the website of the UK government at www.gov.uk. This website provides information on a range of topics related to crime and justice, including statistics on crime rates, information on different types of offenses, and resources for victims of crime. It is a useful resource for anyone who is interested in learning more about crime and justice in the UK.

17   C   In the United Kingdom, you will find signs that indicate areas where smoking is not allowed. These signs are meant to help people identify places where smoking is prohibited and to encourage compliance with the smoking ban. Smoking is restricted in many public places in the UK, including restaurants, bars, and other places of entertainment. By following

these rules, you can help to create a healthier and more pleasant environment for everyone.

18   D   Housing laws are a type of law that deal with issues related to housing and accommodation. These laws may cover a wide range of topics, including disputes between landlords and tenants over issues such as repairs and maintenance, eviction, and the terms of leases. Housing laws are designed to protect the rights of tenants and landlords and to ensure that they are treated fairly in the housing market. They can help to resolve disputes and provide guidance on how to navigate the legal process in cases related to housing and accommodation.

19   D   Several football teams from the United Kingdom compete in European competitions, such as the UEFA (Union of European Football Associations) Champions League. These competitions pit teams from different countries against each other in a series of matches to determine the best team in Europe. The UK is home to a number of successful football clubs that have excelled in these competitions and have garnered a large following both at home and abroad.

20	B	In the United Kingdom, the government is divided into several branches, each with its own specific responsibilities and functions. These include the executive branch, which is responsible for implementing and enforcing the laws and policies of the country; the legislative branch, which is responsible for making laws; and the judicial branch, which is responsible for interpreting and applying the law. Additionally, there are various agencies and departments that carry out specific tasks and serve specific functions within the government.
21	B	The governments of Scotland, Wales, and Northern Ireland are each empowered to pass legislation on certain issues within their respective jurisdictions. These devolved governments are responsible for a wide range of policy areas, including health, education, and the environment, and they have the authority to make decisions and pass laws that affect their respective regions. The central government in London retains authority over certain matters that are considered "reserved" issues, such as foreign affairs and defense.
22	C	There are many law firms and

solicitors' offices located throughout the United Kingdom. Solicitors are legal professionals who provide advice and representation on a wide range of legal issues, including property transactions, criminal defense, and family law. They may work in private practice, in government agencies, or in corporations, and they are regulated by the Law Society of England and Wales, the Law Society of Scotland, or the Law Society of Northern Ireland, depending on where they practice.

| 23 | B | The Citizens Advice Bureau (www.citizensadvice.org.uk) is a UK-based organization that provides free, independent, and confidential advice to people on a wide range of issues, including employment, debt, housing, and legal matters. If you are seeking the name of a solicitor who specializes in a particular area of law, you can contact the Citizens Advice Bureau for assistance. They can provide you with the names of local solicitors who have expertise in the area you are interested in, as well as information about the services they offer and how to contact them. |
| 24 | A | Solicitors are qualified legal professionals who provide advice |

and representation to individuals and organizations on a wide range of legal issues. They are trained in the law and have expertise in specific areas, such as criminal law, civil litigation, or corporate law. Solicitors can help their clients by providing guidance on how to navigate the legal system, drafting legal documents, and negotiating settlements. They may also represent their clients in court proceedings or at other legal proceedings, such as tribunals or arbitration hearings.

Printed in Great Britain
by Amazon

18877222R00217